FIXIN' TO DIE

FIXIN' TO DIE

A Compassionate Guide to Committing Suicide or Staying Alive

David Lester

Readers can send e-mail about this book and the
issues involved to the author at: david@stockton.edu
(The author may not be able to respond personally
to every reader who writes to him.)

Death, Value and Meaning Series
Series Editor: John D. Morgan

Baywood Publishing Company, Inc.
AMITYVILLE, NEW YORK

Baywood Publishing Company, Inc.
26 Austin Avenue
P. O. Box 337
Amityville, NY 11701
(800) 638-7819
E-mail: baywood@baywood.com
Web site: baywood.com

Library of Congress Catalog Number: 2002035600
ISBN: 0-89503-242-2 (cloth)

Library of Congress Cataloging-in-Publication Data

Lester, David, 1942-
    Fixin' to die : a compassionate guide to committing suicide or staying alive / David Lester.
        p. cm. -- (Death, value, and meaning series)
Includes bibliographical references and index.
    ISBN 0-89503-242-2 (cloth : alk. paper)
    1. Suicide. 2. Suicide--Moral and ethical aspects. 3. Suicide--Psychological aspects. I. Title. II. Series.

HV6545 L4184 2002
179.7--dc21

2002035600

for Bijou

with love

Contents

Acknowledgments

I would like to thank Michael Bonacci, Lauren Meltzer, John Morgan, and my wife Bijou for help in writing this book.

Introduction

CHAPTER 1

The Aim Of This Book

Consider.

You are lying in bed in excruciating pain from a serious, perhaps terminal, illness. Maybe you are suffering from a mental illness which involves chronic and high levels of anxiety and which severely limits your life. Perhaps you are simply tired of the day-to-day hassles of what seems to you to be a meaningless and purposeless existence. As a result, you think about the possibility of killing yourself, and you begin to consider this as a viable option.

What Should You Do?

This book is not concerned with the mechanics of the act of committing suicide—how many of which type of pill to take, etc. This information can be found readily in Derek Humphry's book *Final Exit* and Geo Stone's book *Suicide and Attempted Suicide*.[1]

This book is, instead, a guide to making and carrying out the psychological decision to kill yourself or, if you so decide, to continue living.

Although the choice between suicide and continued living is your decision alone, a decision for which I have no bias as to which path you should choose, by focusing so much on the decision to commit suicide in this book, the book appears to be in favor of the

---

[1] Stone's book surveys the various methods for committing suicide more broadly than Humphry's book, and it is a little more explicit about the physical consequences of using each method. Sometimes it reads more like a forensic science book!

option of suicide. The reason for this is that there are many books and articles written on preventing suicide, but very few written in favor of committing suicide. Consequently, the present book does focus more on the decision to commit suicide than on the decision to continue living.

And if you are wondering why David Lester is writing this book, I'll explain why in the next chapter.

FOR WHOM IS THIS BOOK WRITTEN?

The book is written for anyone who is thinking about committing suicide. I have tried to make the book easily readable and to minimize technical jargon and scholarly references.

However, the book may also prove useful for those who know someone who is thinking about killing him or herself—perhaps a loved one, relative, or friend. This book may help you understand them better and make you a better confidante for them. Why do they want to die? What is their reasoning?

In addition, many of us worry about what the future may hold for us and wonder how we will cope with the stresses that could very easily befall us. For example, how we will cope with the loss of loved ones? What if we ourselves suffer one day from cancer or Alzheimer's disease? Many of my friends bought *Final Exit,* not because they wanted to kill themselves right then, but because they anticipated that they might want to end physical or mental suffering later, in their old age, and they wanted to have a "how-to-do-it" book at hand should that circumstance ever arise. *Final Exit* serves as a safety net for them. This book will serve the same purpose—to have at hand for the future should you decide at a later date that suicide might be a reasonable option.

Over 30,000 people kill themselves each year in the United States, and perhaps a quarter of a million people make an attempt at suicide but survive. In Canada, almost 4,000 people commit suicide each year, and another 3,000 do so in Mexico. These individuals have many friends and relatives (who are commonly called "survivors") who will be shocked and upset by these suicidal acts. So this book is also for survivors—to read and use right now.

Remember, in this book I am not urging you to commit suicide. But neither am I urging you not to kill yourself. I believe strongly that it is no one's place to tell other people how to live their lives—and dying is, after all, a part of life. It is not the role of a writer, such as myself, or a psychotherapist, or even a friend or a lover, to tell *you* what *you* ought to do and what *you* ought not to do. It is your life—you must live it as you think fit.

What I *do* attempt in this book is to shed some light on a subject that could be, indeed *should be,* critically important to you—and that is your own death and how and when you want it to occur. After all, we put much thought in our society into making the entry into life good for the infant. We advise mothers how to make their pregnancy healthy for themselves and the baby, and we try to some extent to make the birthing process a good experience for both the babies and their mothers. If we are concerned about our entry into life, then we ought to be as concerned about our exit from life!

And yes, I do think that suicide can be an appropriate way to die, a good death—which is the literal meaning of the word *euthanasia,* a term which has become loaded with other connotations in recent years. (I will discuss this concept in greater detail in Chapter 4.)

THE ISSUES I WILL DISCUSS

Among the issues I am going to consider in this book are:

What kind of death do you want? What would you consider to be a good way of dying for you?

What is the best way to go about making the decision to commit suicide? How do you weigh the pros and cons?

Must the decision be final?

Can suicide be rational and morally acceptable?

Is committing suicide illegal?

Should you have someone assist you with your suicide?

With whom should you discuss your thoughts of suicide and your decision to kill yourself?

If you decide to commit suicide, how should you deal with your loved ones, relatives, and friends?

Should you have a suicide ceremony?

What if you are thinking about suicide but want help in deciding not to kill yourself?

Most of you have probably not given these questions a great deal of thought. You are probably accustomed to thinking that your own death is not an event that you should be involved in. Perhaps, more importantly, you find that thinking about death, especially your own death, is depressing. Most of us would prefer to ignore the topic completely.

And yet, some day, you may be diagnosed with cancer or some other serious irreversible illness. You may be lying in a hospital or nursing home bed, alone and in great discomfort and pain, and then you will wish you had thought about the manner of your dying and had planned something so that you weren't in the sorry situation in which you find yourself. I recently heard about an acquaintance who had tried to plan for her dying and death, but nevertheless found herself at the age of 94 in a horrible situation. After falling in a nursing home and breaking her hip, she was tied to a bed in a hospital to prevent her from thrashing around from the pain she was experiencing after hip-replacement surgery. She also developed pneumonia. Only because she had communicated her desire to her niece several years earlier in a living will[2] indicating that she wished to avoid being kept alive at any cost after the quality of her life had become too poor, was she able to escape this situation. Her niece persuaded a physician to end her suffering with a lethal injection of morphine—an act which is illegal in the part of the United States in which she lived, but which takes place occasionally nonetheless.

Bear this in mind. Every time we hear or read of a new medical advance to treat an illness such as heart disease, the probability increases that we will live longer and eventually die slowly in old age of painful and degenerative diseases, often abandoned by our children and grandchildren, who may indeed be already fighting over the expected inheritance when we pass on.

Even some of those who have worked professionally to prevent suicide kill themselves when their lives became unbearable. Nico Speijer, a leading psychiatrist in the Netherlands, was devoted to the cause of understanding and preventing suicide. He developed cancer in his 70s, and the strong medication required to control his pain made him fear that he was turning into a "zombie." Speijer decided that he wanted to die with dignity and at a time and place of his own choosing. He did not want to become so debilitated that he was dependent upon others and at their mercy. Finally, in September, 1981, he decided to kill himself. Although Speijer's wife was not ill,

---

[2] And signed the appropriate legal papers giving her niece "power of attorney."

she decided that she did not want to live without her husband. So they committed suicide together.[3]

If you are a counselor involved in suicide prevention, working for example at a suicide prevention center, when a person contacts you, uncertain as to whether to live or die, you assume that he or she called a suicide *prevention* center because of a desire, however weak, to be prevented—to be helped to find other options. But most suicides do not call suicide prevention centers. They are certain that they want to die, and they successfully kill themselves.

Today, counselors and psychotherapists, as well as friends and lovers, law makers and judges, and physicians and psychiatrists, feel free to tell us what we ought to do. On the whole, they tell us that suicide is neither a rational nor an appropriate act, and that we have no right to assisted suicide, that is, to legally ask a physician to prescribe for us a lethal dose of a medication to commit suicide. **I think that this is wrong!**

The task of counselors and psychotherapists should be to help you make up your mind about whether and in what way you want to die and then help you carry out your decision. Let me illustrate my point with a personal analogy from marriage counseling.

Richard, a colleague of mine, went into marriage counseling along with his wife. The counselor saw them together and also individually. One Saturday morning while alone with the counselor, Richard had an insight. He said to the counselor, "You don't care about what is good for me; you care only about keeping this marriage together." The counselor considered this and finally agreed that Richard was correct. Richard then got up and left, and he said to me later, "We both knew at that moment that there was no point in my seeking his help anymore. He didn't care about me!"

Just before my second marriage broke up, I went into counseling with my wife. Our counselor began the first session with a statement something like this: "The first task we are going to tackle is to help the two of you decide what you want to do with your marriage. If you decide to stay together and work on your problems, I will help you do

---

[3] In some cases similar to these, the husband has exerted pressure on his wife to die with him, even though, in my opinion, the wife might have had a good life without her husband. This may not have been the case with Speijer, but I suspect that the wives of Arthur Koestler and Stephan Zweig, for example, were psychologically coerced into dying with their suicidal husbands. Such cases illustrate the usefulness of having a counselor participate in these decisions to help the individuals make good choices.

this. Or, if you decide to divorce, then I will help you with that. I have no stake in your decision. My job is to help you decide what you want to do and then help you accomplish your goals."

Richard's marriage counselor was biased. He assumed that his clients *ought* to stay married. My counselor was concerned, instead, with what my wife and I wanted. She wanted to help us decide what *we* wanted and, once we had decided, to help us carry out that decision.[4]

The decision about killing yourself presents the same problem. Most counselors, relatives, and friends will try to deter you.[5] Only a few will remain unbiased and help you reach your own decision.

The goal of this book, therefore, is to take this latter approach, even though we are dealing with the decision to take your own life. We will answer two key questions:

How to decide whether or not you want to commit suicide?

and

How to carry out your decision?

[4] As it happened, my wife wanted out of the marriage, and so we went our separate ways.

[5] Counselors do have a personal right to disagree with your decision but, in that case, they probably should refer you to a counselor whose moral position does not conflict with yours. For example, a marriage counselor who thinks that homosexuality is immoral should not attempt to counselor a homosexual couple who come for counseling to deal with relationship problems that they are experiencing. That marriage counselor should make his or her moral position clear and help the couple find a marriage counselor who can more effectively help them resolve their problems.

CHAPTER 2

Who Is David Lester And Why Is He Writing This Book?

Some of the motives that led me to write this book are described in Chapter 1. But perhaps it would be useful to talk about myself and my background a little.

I started studying suicide when I arrived in the United States from England for graduate study in 1964. I joined the Department of Psychology at Brandeis University in Waltham, Massachusetts, and I was the last student in the department to be permitted to choose his own topic for study, rather than being assigned as a "servant" to work on the research of a faculty member. I chose suicide.

For my dissertation, I carried out six studies on whether suicide can be viewed as an aggressive behavior, just as murder is viewed as an aggressive behavior. I began my scholarly career playing with ideas and theories.

After a couple of years teaching (at Wellesley College), I was invited to work at the Suicide Prevention and Crisis Service in Buffalo, New York, as Director of Research and Evaluation. Although I trained as a telephone crisis counselor and saw a patient or two in counseling, I was primarily involved in generating research and ideas and getting them published. My employer, Gene Brockopp, and I produced the first book dealing with the problems which arise in counseling by telephone people who are in crisis.

In 1971, I returned to academia, to what is now called The Richard Stockton College of New Jersey, a new college in the New Jersey state system of higher education, where I have taught ever since.

Thus, I am an academic and a researcher, not a therapist or counselor. I started playing with ideas, and I have continued to do so. I like to take an idea and develop it, even if it conflicts with an idea I was exploring last year. To give you an example, I have used a famous case of suicide, Ellen West, reported by Ludwig Binswanger, to argue that her psychiatrist facilitated Ellen's suicide in order to rid himself of a client whom he failed to help. But I have also used the case of Ellen West to argue that suicide might, under some circumstances, be an appropriate way of dying. What do I really believe about the case? I'm not sure—probably both.

I have now written over 70 books and over 1900 articles, mainly on suicide, but occasionally on other topics. I am the most prolific scholar in the field of suicide. And yet I still don't have a good answer to the question of why people kill themselves. The research that has been conducted and the writing that has been done is of interest, but sometimes it seems to me that scholarly activity is similar to games like chess—it is a great deal of fun, but has little practical use.

My main focus over the years, aside from pure scholarly research, has been on evaluating the effectiveness of suicide prevention centers and exploring the usefulness of preventing suicide by making it difficult for people to have access to lethal methods for suicide. I have argued for gun control, fencing in suicide venues such as the Golden Gate Bridge in San Francisco, and restricting the amount of lethal medications given to depressed psychiatric patients, among other things. From 1991 to 1995 I was President of the International Association for Suicide Prevention.

However, from time to time I have written about what would constitute an "appropriate" death (a term which I will define later in Chapter 4) and whether suicide could be considered to be a rational choice (an issue discussed in Chapter 5).

And then, seven years ago, I became ill for the first time in my life. I had a pacemaker implanted to prevent my heart from stopping, as had become its custom, and two months later I had part of my colon removed. I spent two separate weeks in the hospital a few months apart, the first times in my life I had been in a hospital. The experience was, to use a trite phrase, eye-opening.

First, I reacted to these relatively simple procedures with several months of depression and even more months of irritability. This worried me. If my response to these procedures was so strong, how then would I react to a chronic and painful illness such as cancer?

I was also upset by the lack of interpersonal caring (or even the ability to pretend to be caring) on the part of my physicians. They denied that some of the physical side-effects I experienced were the result of the pacemaker and the surgery. I wrote to my cardiologists and suggested that, since they obviously hated talking to their patients, they ought to hire a social worker who would attend to their patients' psychological needs.

It is important to note here that the lack of interpersonal skills on the part of physicians was noted back in the 1960s, and programs were initiated to improve these skills in medical students. Those programs obviously have failed, and I have no higher expectations of any programs that might be established today.

My attitude toward life and death changed after my hospitalizations. Every time I heard or read the news that a new cure had been found for some illness, I realized that now more people would stay alive longer with chronic and painful illnesses. I remembered an elderly patient in the hospital in which I stayed screaming all night, and the nurses having to tie her to the hospital bed. I realized that, one day, that could be my fate. A friend of mine told me the story of her very elderly aunt who had a hip replaced whose case I mentioned in Chapter 1. She tried to plan for a "good" death, but people had initially ignored her desires.

I read accounts, most recently in *Time* magazine, of patients in nursing homes with bedsores so large that bone was visible. I read accounts in medical journals of how well physicians can control pain, but then I read a study that reported that one-fourth of elderly cancer patients in nursing homes receive no pain medication at all! I have been told by medical colleagues that, of course, they can control the nausea that accompanies chemotherapy for cancer, and then I read that even the millionaire golfer, Paul Azinger, had nausea during the chemotherapy for his cancer. If Paul Azinger can't have his nausea controlled, what chance do I have?

And so I began to think more seriously about the quality of life as we age and get closer to death. When Dr. Jack Kevorkian began to assist people to commit suicide, I welcomed the fact that he had forced the issue of assisted suicide into public awareness and debate. However, although I am quite certain that I do not want to die in a hospital, in pain and tied to a bed, I am equally certain that I do not want to die in Dr. Kevorkian's Volkswagen van or in a motel in Michigan with him (or someone like him) by my bedside.

In short, these issues which I will explore in this book stopped being a mere intellectual game and became more of a personal quest.

Yes, I want to help suicidal people to find the help that they need if they don't want to commit suicide. But, I also want to help those, who decide that they have lived long enough, to find an appropriate way of dying, even if that way involves suicide.

Hence this book.

CHAPTER 3

What If You Are Suicidal But Do Not Want To Kill Yourself?

Before embarking on a discussion of suicide as a reasonable option, let me consider the alternative option—staying alive. Since my aim in this book is to help you make an intelligent and informed decision about your life, it is important to explore both options.

Perhaps you are depressed, anxious, or generally distressed, and yet you do not want to kill yourself. Or perhaps you are thinking about killing yourself, but you would like to be talked out of it. What can you do?

LONG-TERM TACTICS

Information

A good tactic in the long run is to learn more about suicide. Information often provides us with a sense of control as we come to understand the problem better.

There are many books which provide information about suicide, many written for the general public. Indeed, I have three recent books myself (Lester, 1989, 1993, 1997). But there are many other books, and you can get a sample of those in print from the online bookstores such as Amazon.com or barnesandnoble.com.[1]

---

[1] Be warned that some of the books listed at these sites are for scholars and may be rather dull for the average reader.

Psychotherapy

The majority of people who kill themselves are suffering from a diagnosable psychiatric disorder, most commonly depression. Thus, seeking long-term treatment for this disorder is a good tactic.

One of the most popular and effective methods of treatment of psychiatric or psychological problems is, of course, medication. The modern antidepressants (such as Prozac, Zoloft, and Paxil) are very effective, and lithium continues to be helpful for those suffering from a bipolar affective disorder (which is more popularly known as manic-depression).

However, medication is rarely sufficient by itself. It is much more effective if it is supplemented with psychotherapy. The leading researcher on manic-depressive disorder, Kay Jamison, who suffers from a manic-depressive disorder herself, takes lithium *and* talks to a psychotherapist.

There are many popular self-help books written to help people suffering from depression and other negative emotions. A book that I often recommend to friends and students is the one I myself have used during rough times: David Burns, *Feeling Good.* New York: Signet, 1981.

It also helps to visit a psychotherapist. Finding a good one is, however, not easy, and by "good" I mean one that is a good fit for you and vice versa. The "Yellow Pages" have lists of psychologists, psychiatrists, and counselors, but finding a good fit is a matter of luck. The best suggestions come from friends who have been in psychotherapy who can tell you whether they liked a particular therapist and something about his or her style.

If you go to talk to a psychotherapist, but you find that it was not helpful, do not give up right away. The therapy might turn out to be useful if you persist with the therapist. Alternatively, it may be that the personal style of the therapist or the system of counseling[2] in which the therapist was trained are not right for you. Try a second or third psychotherapist and see if a different personal style or a different system of counseling does help you.

---

[2] There are a dozen or so systems of counseling and, while some psychotherapists are eclectic in their style, able to use a style which is best for you that day, many stick to one style. The systems of counseling include: psychoanalysis, person-centered therapy, transactional analysis, cognitive therapy, Gestalt therapy, behavior therapy, and reality therapy.

Groups for Survivors

There are people who have been touched by suicide, such as the family members and relatives of those who have committed suicide, who run groups for these "survivors" to help them cope with the loss. These groups are especially helpful because those who lose a loved one to suicide (especially the children of suicides) are at higher risk for committing suicide themselves. In the United States and Canada, survivors are very active in the American Association of Suicidology,[3] and that organization holds an annual meeting for survivors, usually in April.

Survivors groups can be found in other countries. One organization with centers in over 40 countries is Befrienders International, whose center are usually called "The Samaritans." Those centers can usually locate survivors groups locally. The Web site of the headquarters (in England) is www.befrienders.org.

SHORT-TERM TACTICS

For the short-term, that is, getting through the next few days or week, there are two possibilities. The first option is to turn to a good friend who knows something about your crisis and who is prepared to spend time with you. But there are not many friends who will do this—after all, they have their own lives and problems, and they may feel anxious about whether they can help you effectively. Also, when we are depressed, we often feel bad about making demands on others.

In the United States and Canada, as well as some other nations such as the United Kingdom, Hong Kong, and Australia, there are networks of suicide prevention centers or crisis intervention centers which provide crisis counseling by telephone 24-hours-a-day, 7-days-a-week. These services are sometimes listed on the inside cover of the telephone directories and more often in the white or yellow pages—under "suicide prevention" or "crisis intervention"—or you can locate them through the Web sites www.suicidology.org and www.befrienders.org. These services have people, trained in crisis counseling, who can listen to you. Most will help you make short-term

[3] Suite 408, 4201 Connecticut Avenue, NW, Washington, DC 20008. Telephone 202 237 2280. The Web site, with links to crisis counseling centers and survivors groups, is www.suicidology.org.

decisions about what to do,[4] and they know which services could help you with your particular problems. In addition, they sometimes have arrangements with these services so that you can by-pass waiting-lists and talk to a staff person quite quickly.

COMMENT

There are many resources available for those who do not want to kill themselves, resources which can help you in the short-term and in the long-term. What has been lacking are resources which are unbiased, which will help you decide to whether you want to kill yourself or not, and which, if you decide to commit suicide, will aid you. If you cannot turn to Jack Kevorkian, to whom can you turn?[5] This book was written in part to fill that void, but, remember, even though the book is biased in presenting more information about killing yourself than about preventing suicide, in the end it is your decision. It is not the place of others to make it for you, unless you desire them to do so.

The books, Web sites, and organizations mentioned in this chapter can provide you with information and suggest counseling services to contact if you want to talk about your problems. An informed decision is always a better decision and so, the more information you acquire, the more likely you are to make a wise choice.

---

[4] Some services (such as those using the name Contact) provide mere listening and will not make suggestions to you about possible options for you.

[5] There some organizations which may be of help to you. The Hemlock Society (www.hemlock.org) provides information for those wishing to hasten their death. Compassion in Dying (www.compassionindying.org) also does this, and sometimes provides social and emotional support during the dying process. Other "right-to-die" organizations can be found by typing in "right to die" at www.google.com.

Some Points to Ponder

CHAPTER 4

How Do You Want To Die?

We are all going to die. Of this there is no doubt. The critical question we must ask ourselves is, therefore, not "Do we want to die?" but rather "How do we want to die?"

Consider this question. How do *you* want to die?

Think about it. Write it down on the remainder of this page.

Have you ever had fantasies of how you might die? Have you ever had daydreams about dying?

When I was a teenager, I daydreamed about dying in a heroic sacrifice—being gored by a charging bull so that others would live. Or going off to the Belgian Congo (now called Zaire) to fight for the rebels against a totalitarian government.

What are your fantasies of how you might die?

Many people have told me that, when they die, they want to feel no pain and they want to be asleep at home in their own bed.[1] Unfortunately, all of the people who die in car crashes, from horribly painful terminal diseases or at the hands of murderers, perhaps away from home, in the street or in a hospital—that is, *most people*—will not die at home in their own bed, asleep, and without pain.

Most of us do not think about this hard reality until it is too late. As a result, most of us will not have the kind of death we want, and the chances are good that we will have just the kind of death we don't want. Therefore, *now* is a good time to start thinking about your death, whatever your age. How do you want to die? And what would you consider to be a "good" death?

THE CONCEPT OF
AN APPROPRIATE DEATH

When psychologists consider the question of what is a good death, they talk about an "appropriate" death rather than a "good" death. A good death is what "euthanasia" means literally, and the term euthanasia now has acquired a variety of connotations which can upset people—for example, it has become associated with "mercy killing," that is, killing someone to end their misery, not necessarily with their permission or agreement.

My aim is this chapter is to have you think about what a good or an appropriate death would be for you. To help you think about this, I will describe some of the ways in which scholars in the field of death and dying have defined the concept. The list is not exhaustive—I am sure that other definitions can be proposed. I will present you with some possible definitions simply to stimulate your thinking on the issue.

WEISMAN AND HACKETT'S DEFINITION

Although the literature is not very extensive, there are some scholars who have written about the concept of an appropriate death

---

[1] I teach a college course on death, and I asked my last class of students how they wanted to die. For the 22 students in class that day, the most common phrases mentioned were: in their sleep (10 students), when old (8), without pain (6), and quickly (6). For example, one 20-year-old female student wrote: I want to die in my sleep, very peacefully, after a long fulfilled life.

(or dying). In 1961, Avery Weisman and Thomas Hackett wrote an article that brought the concept to the attention of psychiatrists. Weisman and Hackett noted that some of their patients knew, correctly as it turned out, the exact time when they were going to die, and yet faced their impending death without conflict, depression, suicidal ideation, or panic. They did not act like those hexed into death by suggestion (sometimes called "voodoo death"), after which they become hopeless and helpless. On the contrary, Weisman and Hackett's patients knew that death was inevitable and they desired it. For these patients, death was faced peacefully, calmly, and without apparent worry.

After reflecting on their experiences with these patients, Weisman and Hackett proposed four specific criteria for a death (or a dying process) to be considered appropriate.

1. Most importantly, death must be seen as an event that reduces the conflict in your life or as a solution to problems you are facing. (Alternatively, there may be few conflicts or problems in your life.)
2. Death must be seen as being compatible with your conscience— for example, you don't view your death as a cowardly act or as a sin.
3. There must be a continuity of important relationships as you die (for example, dying with your loved ones beside you), or there must be some prospect of the relationships being restored (for example, being reunited with loved ones after you die).
4. Finally, you must sincerely desire death.

Because Weisman and Hackett's criteria for an appropriate death were originally proposed only for deaths from natural causes, they did not include suicide as a possible type of appropriate death. However, I think that a suicidal death can meet each of these four criteria and, therefore, be an appropriate death. You may be facing few problems, or your death from suicide would reduce conflict in your life (criterion 1). Your moral philosophy may enable you to see suicide as an acceptable act (criterion 2). You may expect to be reunited with loved ones after your suicide (criterion 3), and you probably do sincerely desire death (criterion 4).

As I mentioned previously, other writers have proposed different criteria for an appropriate death, and I will list five alternatives, all of which would permit suicide to be viewed as an appropriate death in some circumstances.

THE SIMULTANEOUS OCCURRENCE
OF DIFFERENT KINDS OF DEATH

Richard Kalish has identified four types of death—physical, psychological, social, and anthropological—and his classification suggests another criterion for a death to be appropriate. Let me first define his terms.

Biological death is when your organs cease to function, and clinical death is when your organism itself (as a whole) ceases to function. These two forms of death constitute *physical* death. Biological and clinical death need not coincide in time. For example, it is possible for your organs to keep functioning after your brain has been removed from the body. In this situation, you are clinically dead but biologically alive. In fact, this is what happens when organs are removed from a person who has recently died so that they may be transplanted into others who need them.

You are *psychologically* dead when you cease to be aware of your own self and of your own existence. You do not know who you are nor that you even exist. A person in a coma is presumed to be psychologically dead.

Social death occurs when you accept the notion that, for all practical intents and purposes, you are dead, and you act as if you are dead. In cases of voodoo death, if you believe that you have been hexed and expect to die in a few days, you prepare for death. You may refuse nourishment and lay down in expectation of death. In this situation, you remain conscious, and so you are not yet psychologically dead, and you are certainly not physically dead.

Social death may also be defined from the point of view of friends and relatives. In this situation, you are socially dead when the people who know you act as if you no longer exist. For example, an elderly relative may be put in a home and forgotten, and the family acts as if she or he no longer exists. The relatives of a hexed individual may start grieving and preparing for the funeral.

The final kind of death, *anthropological* death, occurs when you are cut off from the entire community, rather than merely your relatives, and treated as if you no longer exist. The Orthodox Jew who marries a Gentile is anthropologically dead to the Orthodox community. The Orthodox community and the person's family mourn for him just as if he or she were physically dead.

Kalish's four types of death provide a possible criterion for an appropriate death. These four kinds of death can occur at different times in your life. For example, an elderly parent may be put in a nursing home and forgotten about (social death), later fall seriously ill and become so senile that she or he loses awareness of who she or he is (psychological death), and even later finally succumb to her illness (physical death). In some families, a person may be mourned on several occasions.

A death could be considered appropriate when all four of these different kinds of death coincide in time. When they occur at different times, ethical and logistical issues are often raised. For example, when a person is in a coma, the issue of whether or when life support systems should be turned off may be raised. Thus, a person who falls into a coma (psychological death) and physically dies much later could be viewed as having an inappropriate death. The person who is placed in a nursing home and forgotten (social death) does not die an appropriate death. Consider, for example, how you feel about these situations—lying in a coma for several years, kept alive by machines, or abandoned in a nursing home with no friends or relatives to visit and check that you are receiving good medical attention and not being physically abused. In fact, my mother in England dreaded being placed in a home, with her only child, myself, thousands of miles away in America, unable to check that she was being taken care of. She often said that, if she had to move to a nursing home, she would kill herself. Luckily, she was able to live at home except for the final week of her life, which was spent in a hospital, where she died of cancer.

Using this criterion, suicide could be an appropriate death since all four kinds of death can occur at the same time in a suicidal death.

THE ROLE OF INDIVIDUALS IN THEIR OWN DEATH

Some existentialist writers believe that death is appropriate only when you play a role in it. In other words, a person struck down by chance factors, such as lightning, would not have died an appropriate death. Obviously, suicides play a major role in their own death. When discussing the death by suicide of one of his psychiatric patients, Ludwig Binswanger, an existential psychiatrist, believed that only in her manner of death did she "fully exist." For Binswanger, we exist authentically only when we resolve situations decisively by our actions. Binswanger's patient, whom he called Ellen West, was psychiatrically disturbed for most of her life. She was hospitalized on several occasions. Her symptoms dominated her life and restricted her opportunities for growth. In her decision to kill herself, she seemed to be making a choice, and for once she was not overwhelmed by her symptoms or the conflicts underlying her psychopathology. Her choice of suicide was authentic.

In this way, when people play a role in their own deaths by committing suicide, their deaths can be judged as appropriate insofar as they took personal control and accountability for their actions.

PHYSICAL INTEGRITY IN DEATH

Some people feel that a "natural" death is a good death because, in a natural death, the body is physically intact and retains its physical integrity. For example, when a person commits suicide by shooting herself or a murder victim is stabbed to death, the body's physical integrity is lost, and the death may be considered inappropriate. From this point of view, the death of someone whose life has been prolonged by the use of transplants and medical intrusions into the body cannot be appropriate. Only a death from natural causes without medical intrusion may be viewed as appropriate. Suicide could be appropriate under this criterion if a suitable method is used, such as an overdose of sleeping pills for, in this case, the physiological damage to the body is minimal (and perhaps less than is the case in death from such illnesses as cancer).

CONSISTENCY IN LIFESTYLE

If I were to ask you how you expect or would like to die, your response will reflect something about yourself, your personality and your fears, but it may also reflect your lifestyle, a lifestyle which has developed as a result of your inherited tendencies, experiences, personality, successes, and failures. People will typically choose a death that fits with their lifestyle. The passive person may choose to die from a disease or even at the hands of another. The aggressive person may choose to die in a fight or in war. The self-destructive person may commit suicide.

What did you write down on the first page of this chapter? Does it seem to you that the mode of death you chose is consistent with your lifestyle?

A person's death may be appropriate, therefore, if he or she dies in a way that is consistent with his or her lifestyle. For example, Ernest Hemingway's suicide by a firearm in the face of growing medical and psychiatric illness was consistent with the death-defying lifestyle he had cultivated during his lifetime. Hemingway ran with the bulls in Spain, hunted big game in Africa, and sought to be in the front lines with the soldiers in Europe during the Second World War. He risked his life in all kinds of situations. It would be hard to imagine Hemingway dying as a shrunken old man, drooling in a corner of a locked ward in a mental hospital.

Suicide could be viewed as appropriate, then, if it is consistent with the person's lifestyle.

Whenever I think about this particular definition of an appropriate death, I think about my own lifestyle. Earlier I mentioned Weisman and Hackett's observation that some of their patients met death calmly and without anxiety.

A few years ago, I was on my way to a give a talk in Mexico City about euthanasia and assisted suicide. Because the airline on which I was traveling had recently had a plane crash in which all the passengers died, I was more anxious than usual to be flying. After we landed (without incident), I rushed through the airport to meet my hosts and, when I was in their car, I began to worry that I had picked up the wrong suitcase because, in my haste, I had forgotten to check the luggage tag. Perhaps, I had picked up a suitcase that looked just like mine. In fact, I was anxious about one thing or another for most of the trip.

Later, when I stood up to give my talk, I described all of this to my audience and noted that I tend to spend most of my time in a state of mild anxiety, worrying about all manner of things every day. How likely is it, then, that I will meet death without anxiety? I shall probably continue to worry about things, including whether I remembered to change my will and turn the stove off and whether there is a God after all. I am sure that my dying and my death, however caused, will be consistent with my lifestyle. The only way I will not be anxious about dying is if I am in an advanced stage of senility, if I am so sick that my emotions are dulled, or if I am stupefied by medication!

If people have been irrational in their thinking for much of their life, they cannot be expected to be rational when they are dying. If you have raged all your life, then you will probably "rage, rage against the dying of the light," as Dylan Thomas wrote. If you have always been unsure about your decisions in life, then you will probably be indecisive in dying as well.

THE TIMING OF DEATH

Edwin Shneidman (1967) suggested that the timing of our death was an important consideration in defining an appropriate death. Shneidman felt that people are sometimes able to discern that, after a given point, any further life would be a defeat or a pointless repetition. There may be points in time when death seems to be the right thing. For example, the Japanese novelist Yukio Mishima placed great importance on his physical appearance and on his skill as a writer. In 1970, at the age of 45, he thought that he had peaked and that his life from then on would decline. He no longer had confidence in his body or in his writing ability. Mishima killed himself by ritual disembowelment rather than face what to him would have been the shame of defeat.

At certain times in your life, a point may come when death would be appropriate and would complete your life's path (perhaps your life's work). Such a death might even heighten your significance by making your memory more treasured by your family or by posterity. Suicide could be consistent with this criterion.

Once I was on a plane that was trying to land in Buffalo, New York, during a rainstorm. The pilot broke through the cloud cover three times, and we could see that the plane was not over the runway, but off-course. Three times he accelerated and took the plane around in a circle to try to land again. The first time this happened, I asked myself whether this was a good time for me to die. I decided that it wasn't. My wife and I were trying to have a baby, we were both thinking of changing jobs and moving, and my career as a scholar was only in its infancy. It would have been an inappropriate time for me to die. That thought calmed me for the first miss at landing. After the second miss, I panicked like everyone else on the plane.

The next time I was on a plane that was in trouble was during a flight to Colombia. The plane was bumping through a thunderstorm, and all of the passengers, including myself, were scared. Again I asked myself whether this was a good time to die, and unfortunately the answer this time was YES! I had just got remarried, I was happy, my career was fine, and my job interesting. It could go only downhill from there.[2] And I also thought that even if it wasn't *my* time to die, maybe it was the right time for the person sitting across the aisle, and he was going to take me down with him!

COMMENT

The concept of an appropriate death is an important one, and these differing criteria are relevant for the life and death of all individuals. Sometimes our lives seem to be full of forces and events over which we have no control. Powerful others, fate, and chance events have a great impact on our lives. It can, therefore, be satisfying and empowering to exert some control over one of the more important events of our life—the leaving of it.

Each of you should determine what is an appropriate death for you. Does one or more of the definitions above make sense for your death? If not, what other definition would you propose?

Included in the responsibilities of counselors, psychotherapists, and doctors who strive to help people improve their lives, should be the goal of helping patients to die an appropriate death. To do this, the counselor must first be aware of the alternative concepts for an appropriate death, and then must identify what the client believes. If death in one particular manner is more appropriate for a client than death in another manner, then perhaps it is the counselor's duty to allow and to facilitate the client to die in that way.

It is not right to impose our definition of an appropriate death on others. What is right for me is not necessarily right for you. But you can argue against me effectively only if you have thought about this issue ahead of time.

[2] And indeed it did. My wife left me and my career stalled.

CHAPTER 5

Can It Be Rational To Kill Yourself?

If you bring up the possibility of killing yourself with friends, relatives, or counselors, they will usually accuse you of thinking irrationally. That places you on the defensive. You have to try to prove to them that you are thinking rationally. How can you deal with this problem?

Before answering this question, we have to define the meaning of the word rational, especially because everyone who comments on the issue of whether suicide can be a rational choice means something different when they use the word. As in the previous chapter in which I discussed the concept of a good death where I listed some of the criteria that have been proposed, I will present and discuss some of the definitions of rationality that have been suggested.

IS SUICIDE ALWAYS THE RESULT
OF A PERSONAL DECISION?

Before examining whether the decision to commit suicide can be rational, it is interesting to consider whether suicide is always the result of a personal decision. For example, if a schizophrenic hears and obeys a voice that commands him or her to jump from a building and fly[1] and, if he or she obeys, his resulting death is not the result of a decision to kill him/herself.

---

[1] This is called an hallucination.

Let us explore this issue further. Some researchers argue that, if a person's behavior has been caused by physiological processes or experiences of the person over which he or she had no control, then the behavior is not the result of a decision. For example, if a person is schizophrenic because of a genetically programmed defect in the dopamine and norepinephrine neurotransmitters in his brain, then it probably does not make sense to say that he decided to be a schizophrenic. Similarly, if people who have experienced particular kinds of traumatic experiences in childhood (such as having been sexually abused or having a parent who committed suicide) commit suicide, then their suicidal behavior may be seen as a result of these factors which were beyond their control. Their suicide was not, therefore, the result of a personal decision.

The idea that people are not responsible for their behavior is a popular view these days. Murderers are sometimes considered to be "not responsible" for their behavior if they are psychiatrically disturbed. Children who had parents who neglected or abused them may be treated leniently when they commit crimes. Scientists frequently publicize their findings of the role of genes or brain biochemistry in causing psychiatric disorders, drug and alcohol addiction, obesity, homosexuality, etc., enabling people to say, "Don't blame me; it's in my genes."

However, we must bear in mind that, so far, no one has been able to identify any factors that are either *necessary* or *sufficient* for a person to commit suicide. For a factor to be a necessary cause of suicide means that *everyone* who commits suicide must have it. For an experience to be sufficient as a cause of suicide means that *everyone* who experiences it would have to commit suicide.

For example, it appears from research that people who lose a parent in the first 16 years of life (from death or divorce) are more likely to kill themselves than those who do not experience such a loss, but not everyone who experiences such a loss commits suicide. Therefore, loss of a parent is not *sufficient* by itself to cause suicide. Furthermore, many people who have committed suicide did not experience the loss of a parent when they were children or adolescents. Therefore, loss of a parent is not *necessary* for suicide.

Although we know of no necessary or sufficient cause for suicide, researchers have identified some factors that increase the likelihood that suicide will occur, such as psychiatric illness, especially depressive disorders. But even a good predictor such as psychiatric illness is neither a necessary nor a sufficient cause of suicide. Among psychiatric patients with a diagnosis of depressive disorder, only about 15 percent will eventually take their own lives. The other 85 percent will die of natural causes. Therefore, even if a person who committed suicide had a depressive disorder, we cannot conclude that this person's depressive disorder caused that person to commit suicide.

However, even if we were to assume that some day a necessary and sufficient cause of suicide will be identified, let us say a particular physiological dysfunction in the brain, we will find that most suicides will still usually go through an agonizing process of "deciding" if they want to commit suicide or not. Because suicidal people usually feel subjectively that they are making a decision, it is appropriate and interesting to examine the rationality of the decision.

WHAT DOES RATIONAL MEAN?

Rationality refers to the reasonableness of the *premises* or *assumptions* that are used in arguing for or justifying a decision. For example, assume you say, "I have not yet found someone who loves me for myself, and I will never find anyone. I will be unhappy if I never find someone who loves me for myself. I prefer death to a life of unhappiness. Therefore, I will kill myself." People will probably object to your rationale for committing suicide because they think that your assumptions are wrong (that is, your assumptions are irrational or false). They would probably argue that it is not necessarily true that you will never find someone who loves you, or that life without a lover will lead to unhappiness. They are objecting to your assumption "I will *never* find someone who loves me for myself" or the assumption "I *will be* unhappy if I *never* find someone who loves me for myself."

It has been suggested that suicidal people may interpret their experiences differently than nonsuicidal people. When confronted with intolerable circumstances, suicidal people sometimes fail to realize that suicide is not the only way to resolve their problems and that there are several options open to them. They act as if they are wearing blinkers and can see only one solution to their problems—suicide. Furthermore, their hopelessness makes them evaluate their circumstances in an overly negative way and, as a result, they think that there is nothing they can do to make the situation better. In this case, the assumptions of the suicidal person are held to be false.

This issue is dealt with in detail by cognitive psychotherapists who believe that the thinking patterns of all distressed people are irrational. They believe that irrational thinking about events leads to pathological emotions and behavior, whereas rational thinking about events leads to appropriate emotions and behavior.

These ideas were originally proposed by Albert Ellis in his system of psychotherapy called Rational-Emotive Therapy. Ellis described several common irrational thoughts. For example, people may believe that, in order to consider themselves worthwhile, they should be thoroughly competent, adequate, and achieving in all possible aspects of life; or they may believe that certain people are bad, wicked, and villainous and that such people should be blamed and severely punished for their villainy.

David Burns, the author of the book *Feeling Good,* has described more general irrational thinking patterns including overgeneralizing (one single negative event is seen as part of a never-ending pattern of negative events) and catastrophizing (a single negative event is viewed as the worst thing that could ever happen to you).

One way of criticizing this theory is with the use of an analogy. In the United States, a defendant in a criminal trial is innocent until proven guilty, but in France a defendant is guilty until proven innocent. Psychotherapists who view irrational thinking as the basis for pathological emotions and behavior take the French position. They place the burden of proof on you, the client, whom they believe is thinking irrationally. If, after your marriage breaks up, you say, "I will never find happiness with another lover," your psychotherapist asks, "Where is the proof that you will never find happiness with another lover?" You are required to prove your belief. The psychotherapist, who obviously is implying the opposite (that you will find happiness with another lover), is not required to prove his or her belief.

In some cases, people's life experiences confirm their so-called irrational thinking. I have friends who have never found someone to love them and who have never been in a long-term relationship. Some of them are in their 60s and probably will never find someone to love them. Had they made such statements earlier in their life, labeled irrational by Ellis and Burns, they would in fact have ended up being correct! Cognitive psychotherapists cannot know for sure whether the assumptions made by their clients are going to be proven false or true in the future, and so they are not justified in forcing their clients to believe that the assumptions are false.

Finally, it could be argued that rationality is not an absolute notion—no statement is either completely rational or completely irrational. A case in point is provided by *inductive* reasoning. Inductive reasoning is an argument in which your assumptions provide some support, but not absolute support, for your conclusion. Suppose I have been rejected by more than one lover. How many lovers must reject me to meet the criterion for "some support" for the inductive generalization? Conclusions are sometimes judged to be irrational by cognitive psychotherapists because the person drawing them has overgeneralized, but cognitive psychotherapists, like logicians, do not propose how many occurrences permit generalization.[2]

CAN PSYCHIATRICALLY DISTURBED PEOPLE HAVE RATIONAL PREMISES?

Some writers on this topic claim that, because many suicides are psychiatrically disturbed, they could not have been thinking rationally.

There are four types of suicide that people sometimes consider to be rational: suicides carried out for a cause such as martyrdom; suicide as a reaction to a lingering, painful, and incurable illness; suicide in response to the absence of any pleasure in life; and love-pact suicides. Paul Pretzel argued emphatically that suicide could not be rational, even for these reasons. He selected cases of each of the four types of suicide listed above and demonstrated some degree of psychiatric disturbance in the people involved. Pretzel concluded that in each case there were psychiatric factors at work in the motivation of the suicide and, therefore, the suicide was irrational. This approach is biased, of course, because he could just as easily have selected a *nondisturbed* person for each type of suicide.

After they review the evidence concerning the person's psychological state of mind before committing suicide, some psychiatrists claim that almost all of the suicides had been

---

[2] The fact that such inductive reasoning may sometimes lead to false conclusions is not an argument against it. Even though the possibility of drawing false conclusions is inherent in the definition of inductive reasoning, sometimes it is the only form of reasoning available to us.

psychiatrically disturbed. Of course, not all psychiatrists feel this way. In fact, there is so much disagreement among psychiatrists on this issue that estimates of the percentage of the psychiatrically disturbed people in samples of suicides range from 5 percent to 94 percent. Since not all suicides are psychiatrically disturbed, some could have been thinking rationally, even using this criterion for rational thinking.

However, it is quite possible that psychiatrically disturbed people can think rationally. There is a well-known joke that I use in my psychology lectures on mental illness. As a man was driving by a mental hospital, he got a flat tire. He stopped to fix it, and some patients who were walking in the hospital grounds came over to watch him. He removed the nuts from the wheel and put them in the hub cap. As he moved to get the spare wheel, he kicked the hub cap, and the nuts flew into a ditch. He couldn't locate them, and, therefore, couldn't figure out how to put the spare wheel on the car. One of the mental patients said to him, "You could take one nut from each of the three other wheels and use those three nuts to attach the spare wheel."

"That's amazing," the man said. "I would never have thought of that. But how come you did? After all, you're in the mental hospital here."

"I'm here because I'm crazy," the patient replied. "Not because I'm stupid."

Often those who are labeled as psychiatrically ill can function quite well in many areas of their life despite their symptoms. Psychiatric disturbance does not necessarily mean that a person cannot think rationally about some issues.

THE STATISTICAL RARITY OF SUICIDE

Very few people commit suicide. Less than 2 percent of all deaths in the United States are from suicide. Furthermore, only a small proportion of the people who experience a trauma will kill themselves. Even people who are a higher risk for suicide, such as those who are diagnosed with a depressive disorder or those who have previously attempted suicide, do not always go on to kill themselves—only about 15 percent do so. Because suicide happens so infrequently, it is clear that the precipitating conditions can never be considered necessary or sufficient, as I have mentioned previously.

Some commentators believe that, because suicide is rare, it is an irrational decision. This is nonsense. Geniuses are rare, but geniuses (brilliant artists, composers, writers, or scientists) do not think irrationally. Rarity is not a good criterion for irrationality.

WHAT PRECIPITATES A SUICIDE?

Some commentators view suicide as a rational decision when it is committed only as a result of certain circumstances. This sometimes means that the observer thinks that he or she might also have committed suicide under such circumstances. If we think that we might kill ourselves if we were dying of cancer, then suicide under those circumstances seems rational to us. If we would never immolate ourselves on the steps of the U.S. Capitol Building in order to protest injustice, then we would probably view such suicides as irrational. Using this criterion as a basis for judging suicide as rational or irrational is an example of the subjective definition of normality.

When we feel that suicide was precipitated by sufficient stressors, we may view the suicide as *understandable,* a term that some commentators equate with justified and rational. This explains why, in recent years, suicide committed by people dying from painful incurable cancers or AIDS-related infections has been widely viewed as rational. (I will discuss this issue in greater detail in Chapter 6.)

DO UNCONSCIOUS FORCES MAKE
SUICIDE IRRATIONAL?

Some theories of suicide, such as Sigmund Freud's psychoanalytic theory, stress that suicide (and indeed all human behavior) is motivated by unconscious forces. In Freud's theory, the unconscious often contains irrational thinking patterns, and so suicide, motivated as it may be by unconscious forces, may be considered to be irrational. However, there is no empirical evidence that unconscious thinking is always irrational. Freud may have asserted that it is, but that does not prove that it is. One of Freud's original colleagues, Carl Jung, believed, in contrast to Freud, that the unconscious could be a source of wisdom and creative ideas, and he encouraged people to tap into their unconscious (through studying their own dreams and through meditation, for example) in order to benefit from its wisdom.

Furthermore, George Kelly, who proposed an alternative theory of human behavior, has argued that psychologists usually claim that behavior is motivated by unconscious forces only when they cannot understand the person's behavior; the psychologist's ignorance is reinterpreted as the patient's unconscious. Kelly, therefore, denied that the unconscious was useful as an explanation of human behavior.

OTHER DEFINITIONS OF RATIONALITY

Clearly, the word rational is used in many ways and, when attempting to evaluate whether suicide is a rational or irrational behavior, it is important to distinguish the various meanings and to explore the implications of each. I have already discussed rationality in terms of psychiatric disorder, necessary and sufficient causes, and unconscious motivation. Other viewpoints are also possible.

Empirical Judgments of Rationality

One way to evaluate whether or not suicide is a rational act might be to look at its outcome. For example, if a suicidal action changes the person's life for the better, perhaps it was a rational action. Certainly, as Nietzsche is commonly quoted as saying, the thought of the possibility of suicide helps many people get through a crisis. You may think, "If things get worse, I do have a way out—I have the option of killing myself." This thought may give you enough energy and motivation to live another day during which the strength of your suicidal impulse may decrease. To take another example, one patient who was assured that no one would interfere if she tried to kill herself, decided not to do so since now she felt in control of her life.

Those who attempt suicide (and survive) are sometimes pleased with the changes in interpersonal relationships brought about by their suicide attempt. But can we say that completed suicides (those who succeed in killing themselves) ever change their lives for the better? This of course depends on how one evaluates the quality of life that the suicidal person was leading as compared to death. Was death worse than life in a concentration camp under the Nazis? In fact, surprisingly few inmates of those camps committed suicide. Perhaps they viewed their life as better than death. Yet those who did commit suicide must presumably have viewed death as better than continued life. The judgment here is subjective. Each individual makes their own decision as to which is better—continued life or death.

Autonomous Individuals May Be Rational

Autonomy refers to the right of people to live their lives and behave in any noncriminal way they choose. In most cases, psychiatrically disturbed people, the retarded, children, and those experiencing extreme stress are viewed as being unable to act autonomously because their judgment is impaired.

Autonomous Americans have the legal right (upheld by the United States Supreme Court) to refuse medical treatment. Such a refusal by an autonomous person may be considered to be a rational choice, at least in the eyes of the law. Because autonomous Americans also have the legal right to commit suicide (suicide is not illegal in America), suicide may likewise be considered rational in the eyes of the law.

Rational versus Emotional Suicide

Some commentators contrast rational suicide (which they define as carefully planned and carried out without emotion) with emotionally-laden and impulsive suicide. Can suicide be the action of a calm and unemotional person? Probably. For example, some suicides by terminally-ill individuals may meet this criterion.

As far as we can tell, Freud's own physician-assisted suicide may well be a case in point. Freud had suffered from cancer of the mouth and jaw for many years, and, after his escape from the Nazis in Austria and his arrival in England, the ulcers grew worse and the pain more severe. He had arranged for his physician, Max Schur, to inject him with a lethal dose of morphine when the suffering became too great to bear, and in September 1939, Freud died when Schur followed these instructions. (Even in his physician-assisted suicide, Freud was ahead of his time!)

There are no data on the relative frequency of emotional and nonemotional suicides, and so we do not know what proportion of suicides may be considered rational according to this criterion.

An Economic View of Suicide

Economists define rational behavior as one that maximizes some variable such as utility (which we may loosely define as satisfaction) or profit. Can suicide ever be rational using the criteria of economists? Bijou Yang (my wife) and I have presented a cost-benefit analysis of suicide in which we assumed that individuals weigh the costs and benefits of suicide as compared to the costs and benefits of alternatives to suicide. From this economic viewpoint, suicide may maximize individual utility for the individual; that is, the benefits may outweigh the costs.

In psychoanalytic theory, desires (both conscious and unconscious) motivate all behavior, and all behavior is a compromise of conflicting desires. Thus, choices in this perspective can always be seen as satisfying desires and, therefore, maximizing psychological utility. The fact that some of the desires may be unconscious has no relevance to this criterion.

It should be noted that there can also be a discrepancy between our short-term goals and our long-term goals. When these goals conflict, we may appear to be making poor decisions. Edwin Shneidman once noted that suicide could be seen as a permanent solution to a temporary problem, meaning that suicide was satisfying a short-term goal, but not necessarily a long-term goal, for the person. When our short-term and long-term goals are consistent, our decisions seem to be more rational.

Does The Decision To Commit Suicide
Follow Rational Laws?

In a recent study, I presented college students with a scenario in which they had AIDS. Each student was given a different level of pain and a different probability of surviving for one year. The students then had to estimate the probability that they would commit suicide.

I found that the more severe the pain, the higher the estimated probability of suicide; also the greater the probability of death within one year, the higher the estimated probability of suicide. Thus, the estimated probability of suicide by the students followed meaningful psychological laws. Their estimated probabilities of committing suicide made sense. Their decisions could, therefore, be considered rational.

Some commentators believe that it is irrational for psychiatrically depressed people to commit suicide. I disagree; suicide for these individuals follows a meaningful psychological law and, therefore, it is rational. On the other hand, if non-depressed people were found to be more likely to kill themselves than seriously depressed people, that would not make sense to me, and I would judge the behavior to be irrational.

IS IT ILLOGICAL TO KILL YOURSELF?

Haven't I just answered this question?

No. The problem of illogicality is different from that of irrationality, and many people confuse *logic* with *rationality*. Rationality refers to the truth of the *premises* (or the assumptions) used in reasoning. Logic may be defined as the study of reasoning. An *argument* is a set of statements that result in a conclusion that is implied or supported by the premises. Good arguments are considered to be *valid*. If the premises are true, then the conclusion must be true. For example, the following is a valid argument:

all cats are animals
this is a cat
therefore, it is an animal

What does an unsound argument look like? An example might be:

I am a man
Jesus Christ was a man
Therefore, I am Jesus Christ

The first two statements (the premises) are correct, but the conclusion is false.

Some people, including mental health professionals, believe that people who kill themselves were not thinking logically when they made the decision to commit suicide. However, if we grant the premises of suicidal people, there is no evidence that their reasoning is unsound.

The only research I could find which claims that suicidal people are thinking illogically is by Edwin Shneidman and Norman Farberow in which they described what they called a *psychosemantic fallacy*. They suggested that some suicidal people seem to confuse "the self as experienced by themselves" with the "self as experienced by others." A problem occurs in their reasoning when the person assumes that these two "selves" are the same. For example, a suicidal individual may reason as follows: I know that when people kill themselves, they get attention from others; therefore, if I kill myself, I will get attention from others. The "I" that kills is the self as experienced by the self while the "I" that gets attention is the self as experienced by others. These two selves are not the same. The person who kills himself will not be able to experience the attention he seeks after he is dead because the self as experienced by the self no longer exists.

After being rejected by my girl-friend in my college days, I fantasized about killing myself and watching her standing at my grave, regretting that she had spurned me. I then realized that, of course, if I were dead, I would not be around to see her anguish. Luckily for me, I did not fall prey to the psychosemantic fallacy!

Shneidman and Farberow pointed out that the psychosemantic fallacy does not apply if the suicidal individual believes that there is a life after death, because in that case he may be able to reap the benefits of suicide by observing the reaction of friends and relatives.

Aside from this possibility, scholars have never demonstrated that the reasoning behind suicide is illogical. So, if you are considering suicide, you are probably thinking logically.

COMMENT

If you talk about your desire to commit suicide, your friends and relatives may well try to convince you that you are being irrational or illogical. What I have tried to do in this chapter is to lay out a set of definitions to address the question of whether suicide can be rational and to give you arguments to counter the opinions of your friends and relatives.

Irrationality can be interpreted as: 1) the degree to which an individual is psychiatrically disturbed; 2) the statistical rarity of a behavior; 3) whether there are sufficient precipitating events and "causes" identified for the suicidal act to enable us to see the act as understandable; 4) whether there are unconscious processes motivating the behavior, at least in part; 5) whether the behavior improves the state of the person; 6) whether the behavior is that of an autonomous individual; 7) whether the decision is affected by emotional states; 8) whether the behavior maximizes utility; 9) whether we ourselves would commit suicide for the same reasons; and 10) whether suicidal behavior follows meaningful psychological laws. Of course, some of these criteria might be judged more relevant to the decision to commit suicide than others.

Obviously the act of suicide can be irrational. The critical question is whether some suicides can be rational. Some researchers report that many suicides do not have a psychiatric illness, and some suicides meet the criteria for being autonomous individuals. Occasionally a suicide does seem to improve a person's situation and maximizes utility (both for the suicide and the society). And, unless one thinks that suicide is never acceptable for any reason, most of us could probably find acceptable reasons for killing ourselves. Furthermore, there may be some suicides whose assumptions are true or, at least, not demonstrably false. On these grounds, the act of suicide can be rational.

On the other hand, suicide is always statistically rare and, if one accepts the existence of the unconscious, is probably always motivated in part by unconscious forces.

Recently, I studied the lives of 30 individuals who committed suicide who were interesting and famous enough to have biographies and autobiographies published about them. Did any of these people fit the criteria above? It is difficult to be sure without meeting the person prior to their death and talking to them about their decision. However, several of the suicides did seem to me to be rational using the criteria discussed above. For example, the physician-assisted suicide of Sigmund Freud, who was very old and in the end stages of a painful cancer, met many of the criteria.

So, if someone says to you that your decision to commit suicide is irrational, you do not have to accept their labeling of your decision. You can ask them to explain why they think that your decision is irrational, and their response will indicate which of the criteria discussed above they are using. You can then point out the errors in their views!

CHAPTER 6

Is Suicide A Rational Decision Only If You're Dying?

Some people believe that suicide can be an appropriate decision only for those who are terminally ill—perhaps because it is clear that the quality of life for those who are dying will not improve. If the person is "only" depressed, however, these commentators no longer consider suicide appropriate. They argue that depressed people could find ways other than suicide to eliminate their pain.

In this chapter, I will criticize this position.

THE QUALITY OF LIFE

Some mental health professionals argue that, in an ideal world, everyone ought to be prevented from committing suicide, regardless of the circumstances of the case and their reasons for wanting to die. In an ideal world, everyone with psychological problems would be able to receive and benefit from effective psychotherapy and medication. There would be no incompetent psychotherapists, there would be no side effects from medication, and there would be adequate medical insurance to cover psychotherapy.

Of course, the world is not ideal. Psychotherapy often does not work, psychotherapists are sometimes incompetent, medication does have side effects, and insurance coverage for psychotherapy is currently being reduced in most health plans. Therefore, I would argue that people who are suicidal may have little reason to expect

43

a better life if they continue living. I do not think that it is irrational for them to expect that circumstances will continue to be bad or get even worse and to decide that there is no other alternative to suicide.

We cannot address the question of whether suicide is a reasonable decision by discussing only the rationality of the act. Evaluating the decision to commit suicide has to take into account the alternatives that are available to each person—suicide versus psychiatric hospitalization, or suicide versus a lingering death from cancer treated by a medical profession that in America still seems to care little for the comfort of the patient. We must consider what the quality of life would be for people in each of the alternatives open to them.[1]

Of course, the issue of who should decide what constitutes an adequate quality of life is a thorny one. Imagine a person whose love relationship has ended. This person may judge the quality of life without the lost love as unacceptable. Someone else may believe that the person will get over the loss and be able to go on to lead a good life. Whose judgment should prevail?

I would argue that each of us is responsible for deciding whether the quality of our own life is satisfactory. If we judge the quality to be unsatisfactory, then it is up to us, and us alone, to decide whether and how to change our existence.

Other people are not able to judge the quality of your life for they are not experiencing what you are experiencing. They view you only through the lenses of their own experiences. What makes each of us unique is that our experiences differ—our own experience is different from the experience of every other person who has ever lived.

Of course, for some people, it can be very helpful to have a counselor assist us in making this decision—if a suitable counselor can be found—for then we could examine in detail all of our desires and thoughts and make a sound decision. The opinions of a neutral, objective outsider can be helpful in this process.

---

[1] Barbara Oskamp, one of the people who fought for the Oregon law permitting assisted-suicide, developed impaired memory as a result of radiation treatment for her inoperable brain tumor. Treatments often have side effects which, for some patients, may be unacceptable.

DEPRESSION AS A REASON FOR SUICIDE

Most of us experience depression in some form. Many of us are mildly depressed from time to time, but usually when the depression lifts, we are happy again. Others, however, are chronically depressed, sometimes quite severely so. Furthermore, many people who are ill or in physical pain are understandably depressed as a result of their condition. Depressed people frequently consider the possibility of suicide, and the majority of suicides are depressed at the time of their death.

Some physicians argue that if we treated the depression of suicidal people, they would no longer be suicidal. For example, they believe that in cases of suicidal people who are ill, treating their depression would make them less suicidal despite their ongoing illness or pain.

Unfortunately, when psychiatrists recommend treating the depression of suicidal people, their plan is usually to prescribe medication. They often do this in a cold, impersonal manner, with little or no discussion of the side effects of the medication and without taking time to get to the know their clients and providing counseling.

Many years ago, at a conference where I was discussing Ernest Hemingway's suicide, I mentioned the possibility that the electroconvulsive therapy he received for his psychiatric disorder may have played a role in his suicide because it eliminated many of his memories. Memories are important for everyone, and especially so for an autobiographical writer like Hemingway. Hemingway was experiencing writer's block toward the end of his life, and loss of memory may have made it worse. Hemingway first tried to kill himself as he was being taken to the Mayo Clinic for a second course of electroconvulsive therapy, and he successfully took his life the next morning at home after being released from the hospital.

I was criticized by several psychiatrists for suggesting that electroconvulsive therapy caused memory loss. However, a few years later, several first-person accounts and scholarly articles documented that permanent memory loss, sometimes severe, can indeed follow electroconvulsive therapy! Were those psychiatrists who had criticized me earlier ignorant or liars?

Psychiatrists like to treat depression with medications, and they often avoid exploring the life situation of their clients and providing more general counseling. For severe depression (technically called a major depressive disorder), the treatment of choice is a modern antidepressant, such as a serotonin reuptake inhibitor (SRI). Medications have side effects that physicians often fail to discuss with their patients. Some side effects are common, others are rare. One potentially serious side effect of SRIs is impotence. A recent advertisement in *Time* (July 21, 1997) stated that sexual desire was decreased in only 4 percent of those who take these medications; but, in an article in *Psychology Today* (July/August, 1997), a psychiatrist estimated that more than half of patients taking such antidepressants develop sexual problems. One of my colleagues in the field of suicide studies told me that he personally would find it difficult to choose between being less depressed but impotent or being more depressed but with undiminished sexual activity. I doubt that I am in the minority when I too say that I don't relish the idea of having my sexual interest or ability diminished by medication. Maybe some of my original depression would be alleviated by taking the antidepressant, but I'd certainly have a new reason for being depressed if it made me impotent!

While I was at a conference on suicide a few years ago, a colleague of mine, a psychiatrist, noticed that I was depressed and advised me to take an SRI. Even he, a friend, did not warn me about the possible side effects and neither did he bother to find out why I was depressed.

For those who have a bipolar affective disorder (more commonly known as manic-depression), Lithium is the treatment of choice. Many patients consider Lithium to be a miracle medication. It moderates their mood swings and makes life seem worth living. Others, however, hate its effects. People report that Lithium makes them unable to feel the "highs" and that it impairs their creativity.

Abbie Hoffman, the well-known activist, tried Lithium for his bipolar affective disorder but disliked the side effects and discontinued taking it. He then tried Prozac and Valium, but I guess neither helped him enough for he went on to commit suicide. Incidentally, perhaps had Hoffman been able to discuss his decisions about his medication with a counselor, as I have suggested in Chapter 12, he would have been better served. He might have still made the same choice, but counseling would have allowed him to make a more informed decision.

Anne Sexton, the American poet and Pulitzer prize-winner, was prescribed an antidepressant (Imipramine) and a phenothiazine for her psychiatric disorder. She disliked the side effects of these medications, claiming that they destroyed her creativity as a poet and made her uncomfortably sensitive to the sun. She often refused to take them, evidently finding her depression to be the lesser of two evils. Eventually she too committed suicide.

Many years ago, when my first marriage was breaking up, I went to my physician because I had a fever. He noticed that I was depressed and gave me several bottles of antidepressants from his drawer. (Incidentally, he gave me enough for a lethal overdose!) After taking one of the pills, I went off to a meeting. Once there, I wrote a note to a colleague and, when I was done, I realized that I could not recognize my own hand writing. It had become tiny. Then another colleague asked for my opinion about an issue that the group was discussing. It took me 30 seconds (although it seemed like 10 minutes) to tell him that I had no opinion. I decided right then and there to stop taking the antidepressant. Since I had no intention of taking the antidepressant daily for the rest of my life, I would live the rest of my life with my normal state of consciousness. Consequently, I wanted to make the critical decisions in my life while in that normal state, not drugged with a medication.[2]

THE ROLE OF PAIN

The reason for discussing the issue of pain in a book on suicide is that most people cannot stand it—the actual agony of the experience of pain, the thought that it may increase in intensity, and, even worse, knowing that it may never abate.

In my opinion, the way that physicians manage pain in the United States is deplorable. When I hear physicians claim that they can control their patients' pain and remove it completely, I distrust them because I continue to hear of cases of patients in severe pain that is not being controlled, let alone alleviated. If physicians can alleviate pain, then why are they not willing to do so?[3]

---

[2] Because of my feelings about the inept way most physicians and psychiatrists communicate and choose to deal with their patients, I now prefer the idea of *counselor-assisted suicide* as opposed to physician-assisted suicide. A physician is the last person I would want to assist my suicide, except perhaps to write me a prescription for a medication with which to overdose. I would want a counselor or psychotherapist to talk to me and to my significant others.

[3] The same is true for claims that physicians can eliminate the nausea that accompanies chemotherapy for cancer.

In England, the medical community is much more humane in alleviating pain, and they are less concerned about the possibility that their patients may become addicted to the pain-killing medication. My mother, who died from cancer, was under the care of a doctor who gave her large quantities of morphine to take for her pain. He allowed her to choose the dose that she felt worked best for her. She had so much morphine in her apartment that she could easily have used it to commit suicide, but she chose not to. She found that, if she took enough morphine to kill the pain completely, she tended to stumble when she walked. In fact, she did fall once, fracturing a rib, so she lowered the dose so that she could walk without falling, even though she experienced some pain from the cancer. The important lesson here is that her doctor allowed *her* to make the decisions about what was important to her. He did not refuse to help her; nor did he impose his views on her.

People have complained about the interpersonal skills of American physicians for years, and I read from time to time that efforts are being made during their training in medical school to improve their performance in this area. As I mentioned earlier, after being hospitalized twice in 1995, I concluded that no progress has been made in this area. My cardiologist and internist were superb technicians, but they were completely devoid of any interpersonal skills that would enable them to relate to me as a person with feelings.

Is my experience untypical? Are my opinions biased? Felicia Cohn and her colleagues at George Washington University recently observed in an article in *The Chronicle of Higher Education*, "Dying patients are not receiving the care they need, and physicians are not prepared to provide it." They argued that physicians are too concerned with the aggressive treatment of disease and that they pay little attention to the care they are supposed to provide for patients who are dying. Cohn suggested that changes in medical school programs might alleviate this problem. That sounds fine, but I read proposals for similar changes 30 years ago. Clearly, there has been little progress if the same proposals are being put forward today.

Recently, there has been a spate of articles and letters in the media about this problem. In a letter to *The Philadelphia Inquirer* on July 4, 1997, Mary Anne Saathoff, President of the Fibromyalgia Alliance of America, wrote, "Those with severe and unrelenting pain . . . all too often search in vain for a physician who will prescribe adequate pain-relieving techniques and medications."

On July 6, 1997, in the same newspaper, Robert Calica wrote on the Op-Ed page, "The number of terminally ill Americans suffering intolerable physical pain, personal degradation and family trauma is directly attributable to medical advances"—advances that Calica says result in physicians prolonging the life of patients, subjecting them to more suffering than they would have experienced had the disease run its natural course.

I was in the library recently catching up with the latest articles on suicide, when I was struck by the titles of several recent papers, such as

> "Michigan moves toward better pain management," and "MSMS, AMA take proactive stance—advocate quality pain management techniques."

This recent spate of articles indicates that the medical establishment did little in the past to ease the dying of patients until confronted with the growing public demand for assisted suicide. Each assisted suicide is a strong statement to the medical community that the profession has failed us.

In my opinion, the current state of the medical profession, combined with the move toward HMOs for insurance coverage of illness, will ensure that dying patients will continue to suffer in the future.

Why is it that American physicians are so reluctant to relieve the pain of their patients? Perhaps it is partly the result of the aversion of physicians to dying patients, since such patients represent their "failures" and arouse their own anxieties about dying and death. As a result, they ignore and avoid their dying patients. Their reluctance is possibly a result also of the anxiety of Americans about drug addiction. What if terminally ill patients were given enough morphine and for a long enough period of time that they became addicted? In fact, providing adequate pain medication does not always result in addiction. And even if it did, what harm is done if the terminally ill die addicted? It seems that the medical establishment believes that it is more appropriate to let patients die in pain rather than become addicted!

ARE THERE ANY WRONG REASONS FOR COMMITTING SUICIDE?

Since many supporters of assisted suicide think that it is appropriate only for dying patients, it seems that other reasons for committing suicide are considered to be inappropriate. Is this a reasonable position?

While everyone is entitled to their own opinion, we cannot judge whether an action taken by another person is right or wrong for them and, when discussing something as personal as suicide, all that matters are the subjective feelings of the person concerned.

Every person looks at things differently and, of course, it is the same with suicide. Each of us has our own circumstances under which we would judge suicide to be a right or reasonable course of action. Would I kill myself over a failed love relationship? I've had several, but I didn't commit suicide. In other words, for me, a failed love relationship is not a sufficient cause for me to kill myself. But that does not mean I think that someone who did or would kill himself over a failed love relationship had made a "wrong" or "bad" decision. I am not living their life; I do not experience their pain; and therefore I cannot possibly know how they feel.

The inmates in the Nazi concentration camps during the Second World War all reacted differently to their situation. Some inmates gave up on life and killed themselves; many got themselves killed by the guards in what may be considered to be an indirect form of suicide; others decided to cling to life, some ultimately surviving the camps. Of this latter group, a few went on to commit suicide later when they were faced with the general problems of life that all of us face. When Bruno Bettelheim, the mental health pioneer who worked with disturbed children, committed suicide as an old man in a nursing home in Maryland, many of us said, "But he survived a year in a concentration camp. How can old age be worse than that?"

In a similar sense, I cannot imagine what it must be like to suffer from schizophrenia—the anxiety and the mental suffering involved—and so I will not judge as inappropriate the suicide of a person who does not want to experience another episode of this disorder.

We cannot evaluate the pain experienced by others.

Suicide, when suffering from a terminal illness, has come to be viewed as rational probably because a good proportion of Americans would consider suicide under that circumstance. The law passed by the state of Oregon in the 1990s (and updated in 1998) which permits assisted suicide is quite restrictive in its application. It requires that applicants for assisted suicide be terminally ill (within six months of death), and their judgment must be unimpaired by depression or a psychiatric disorder. Interestingly, the Oregon Medical Association opposed the law when it was first proposed. This seems to me to be further evidence that physicians have little compassion for their patients!

Individuals with relentless physical or mental pain and anguish from any cause—what Edwin Shneidman has called *psychache*— should have the right to decide whether or not they want to die, and their decisions should be respected. Furthermore, it would be ideal if there were counselors to assist them with making an informed decision. Unfortunately, this is not possible at the present time.

CHAPTER 7
Isn't Suicide Immoral?

Most major religions consider suicide a sin or a tragically mistaken action, and this moral judgment causes much distress to those who believe in these religions but who are, nevertheless, thinking about killing themselves.

The moral question is easily highlighted for there are two major ways of deciding this issue, namely absolute principles and the utilitarian approach.[1]

ABSOLUTE PRINCIPLES

Many people subscribe to absolute principles, and they often adopt those of the religion that they follow. One absolute principle in the Christian religion is "Thou shalt not kill," and this usually means that Christians do not approve of capital punishment, abortion, or suicide.

One problem with absolute principles is that people do not always apply them consistently in all situations. Those firmly opposed to abortion and capital punishment often go off to war quite willingly, sometimes believing that "God is on our side." But if you break an absolute principle in any way, then it is no longer an absolute principle.

Another problem with absolute principles is that they can conflict with one another. For example, "Thou shalt not kill" conflicts with

---

[1] In moral philosophy, the use of absolute principles is known as duty ethics (or deontology) and the utilitarian approach as teleological ethics.

the *principle of autonomy,* which asserts that autonomous individuals have the right to behave in any noncriminal way they choose. One difficulty here is agreeing upon who is autonomous. As mentioned in Chapter 5, this label is typically not granted to the psychiatrically disturbed, the retarded, children, and those suffering from extreme stress. This is why federal courts typically grant adults the right to refuse medical treatment if their religion forbids it, but will authorize such treatment for their children.

In effect, the principle of autonomy permits autonomous individuals to kill themselves if they so desire. As one author titled his recent article, "It's my body, and I'll die if I want to."

THE UTILITARIAN APPROACH

The alternative approach to finding an absolute principle to guide your life is the *utilitarian* position. In a utilitarian sense, something is moral if it tends to maximize good and minimize harm. The problems here are twofold. First, judgments of good and harm are subjective, and different people weigh them differently. Second, the question arises of good and harmful for whom—the individual, one's family and friends, or the society as a whole?

People often worry about the harm caused to others by an individual's suicide; in totalitarian systems of government, the potential harm to society has been used to argue against the acceptability of suicide. It is interesting to note that this issue is rarely raised, and certainly never applied, to those about to marry or about to have children. There is no legal mechanism in our society to prevent a spouse abuser from getting married or an actual or potential child abuser from having children.

My opinion is that the decision to commit suicide should be decided simply on the basis of what is best for ourselves[2]—a utilitarian approach. In order to minimize the harm to others, our loved ones should be involved in the process, perhaps even in the decision-making phase, hopefully before but certainly after the decision has been made, so that they can begin to work through their feelings prior to the suicidal person's death.

---

[2] In this, I am showing a Western bias, a bias that emphasizes the self over others. In many non-Western cultures, the individual is viewed as part of a larger network, and the benefit for the society outweighs the benefit for the self.

If the right of individuals to kill themselves is recognized by society, then there will be ample time for concerned relatives and friends to meet with the suicide-to-be in order to communicate with one another and work through their emotions and conflicts before the suicidal death occurs. This process will ease the pain of the survivors.

WHAT ABOUT RELIGION?

The fact that suicide is viewed as a moral wrong by many faiths leads some suicidal individuals to change their religious philosophy in order to justify their choice of self-destruction to themselves and to their loved ones. They may stop attending church or become agnostics or even atheists. They may seek to find evidence that God forgives everything, including suicide. They may argue that God will understand their unique situation and forgive them. They may persuade themselves that even Hell will be better than their present life on earth, or they may come to believe in reincarnation.

In order to cope with the moral judgment that religions place on suicide, people about to kill themselves often try to justify their choice, and their efforts can be sometimes observed in the suicide notes they leave. In their notes, the writers usually beg forgiveness or request indulgence, and they communicate that they are fully aware of what they are doing even though they know that others will not necessarily understand their reasons.

Jerry Jacobs has noted a variety of statements in suicide notes that serve these purposes. The note writers may ask God for forgiveness and request others to pray for them. They may make it clear that they are faced with extremely distressing problems. This state of affairs usually is presented as part of a long history of distressing crises, and not simply as one isolated crisis. They often indicate that death is the only solution possible, and they may relate how they have come to feel socially isolated so that they cannot talk about this distress with others or turn to others for comfort and support. These writers may define their problems as not of their own making, and they may try to take measures which they hope will spare them from Hell.

Those of you who are conventionally religious and who believe in a faith which condemns suicide should take time to consider these issues as you move toward reaching your decision.

CHAPTER 8

Assisted Or Unassisted Suicide?

There has been an enormous amount of controversy about assisted suicide in recent years, stimulated in large part by the assistance provided to suicides by Jack Kevorkian. Kevorkian helped many people commit suicide, and several physicians have publicly admitted that they have had a role in hastening the death of some of their patients in the past.

Let us look at some of the issues surrounding assisted suicide.

PRESCRIBING VERSUS INJECTING MEDICATIONS

When Sigmund Freud decided to end his life in 1939, he had his physician inject him with a lethal dose of morphine, a quick and painless way to die. The Oregon assisted suicide law which was recently passed does not allow physicians to inject a client with a lethal medication. The law permits a physician to prescribe a lethal overdose to people who are terminally ill and who are not depressed or psychiatrically disturbed, but the clients must administer the overdose themselves.

This difference is of great importance. First, let us look at it from the physicians' point of view. The kind of person who becomes a physician usually wants to fight disease and illness, to save life, not hasten death. It is, therefore, reasonable that some physicians may object to assisting suicide.

In surveys that have been conducted on hospital staff of their views on the subject of life support for dying patients, most of them report that they find it much harder to turn off a switch or to pull a plug from its electrical socket than to let the battery run out that is running a life support system. The former seems more like actively "killing" someone while the latter seems more like "letting someone die." Letting someone die causes less emotional distress and results in less guilt for the staff.

This distinction is important in discussions of euthanasia (which literally means a "good" death), and the two styles are sometimes labeled active and passive euthanasia. These terms correspond to the familiar distinction between acts of commission and omission—actions you carry out versus actions you fail to carry out. In moral philosophy, sins of commission are commonly thought to be more serious than sins of omission.

WHY DO SOME PEOPLE WHO WANT TO DIE WANT SOMEONE ELSE TO KILL THEM?

In the United States, about 30,000 people kill themselves each year—that is, without the help of someone else. The Hemlock Society, which published Derek Humphry's book on how to commit suicide, *Final Exit*, will not help people kill themselves, but they will provide helpful information on how people can do it themselves. Why is it that some people want others to participate in their suicide, in preparing the medication or arranging the apparatus? Even Freud, a physician who could easily have injected himself with morphine, wanted his physician to do it for him. Possible explanations include lack of knowledge, physical inability, and the personality traits of the potential suicide.

Lack of Knowledge

Some people lack the knowledge to kill themselves. In addition to the 30,000 people who will kill themselves in the United States this year, it is estimated that about eight times as many will attempt suicide but survive the attempt—that is, about 240,000 people. It is true that many attempters do not really intend to die, but there are many others who do want to die and yet fail. Many of the failed attempts of those who really do want to die occur because sometimes people are ignorant about methods of causing death. For example, the use of simple pain killers is a common but ineffective method. Aspirin is too mild a poison, and often people vomit up the aspirin. Tylenol is also mild and can cause severe kidney damage rather than death.

A perusal of the medical literature on attempted suicide illustrates the varied ways in which people injure themselves seriously as a result of unsuccessful attempts to kill themselves. Plastic surgeons publish reports on the restoration to some semblance of normality of faces shattered by bullets. Burn specialists work to heal the skin of those who failed to die from self-immolation, and many patients live painful lives as a result of the severe internal damage inflicted by the overdoses they took. Self-inflicted gunshot injuries result in colostomies, brain damage, seizures, and amputations. People who try to jump to their death but survive are sometimes left with spinal cord injuries, resulting in paralysis.

Physical Inability

Some potential suicides no longer have the physical ability to kill themselves. They may not be able to leave the house to fill a prescription or purchase a gun. Because of weakness or paralysis, they may be unable to leave their bed. Percy Bridgman, a Nobel Prize winner in physics, was suffering from Paget's disease which was causing severe pain. He was slowly losing mobility in his limbs, and he was unable to find a physician to end his life. He killed himself just before he would have been physically unable to do so. In his suicide note, he said:

It isn't decent for Society to make a man do this thing himself. Probably this is the last day I will be able to do it myself. P.W.B.

Lynne Lennox committed suicide on July 2, 1997, in a motel near Detroit, apparently assisted by Jack Kevorkian. She had suffered from multiple sclerosis for many years, and her illness had eventually forced her to quit work as a bookkeeper. Her mother was quoted as saying, "She couldn't do anything for herself," and Lennox left a videotape describing how the illness had left her unable to walk and forced her to wear diapers. Such people may need another person willing to engage in an act of commission, in order to commit suicide. Others do not require the help of others, and yet still desire someone to act as the agent of their death. Why?

Personality Type

Psychologists have published a great deal of research on an aspect of personality that we call belief in a "locus of control," which can be either external or internal. Some people believe that what happens to them is a result of powerful other people or fate (an external locus of control), while other people believe that they themselves are responsible for what happens to them (an internal locus of control). For instance, if you have been in a car crash, do you blame yourself ("Why was I so careless?"—an internal locus of control), the other driver ("Why didn't he pay better attention to the traffic?"—an external locus of control), or fate ("As soon as I got out of bed today, I knew it was my unlucky day!"—also an external locus of control)?

Psychologists usually consider an internal locus of control to be psychologically healthier than an external locus of control, because an internal locus of control means that we can do something about the situation. If what happens to us is the result of luck or fate or the behavior of others, then it is harder for us to bring about changes.

Individuals who choose to commit suicide by themselves may have an internal locus of control, while those who want others to kill them may want to avoid responsibility for their own death, consistent perhaps with having an external locus of control.

This is not necessarily bad. Remember that one definition of an appropriate death is that the manner of dying is consistent with your lifestyle. People who believe in an external locus of control may prefer to have others take responsibility for their death—or they may prefer to die in a self-destructive but nonsuicidal way, such as by provoking someone else to murder them or by playing Russian roulette and letting luck determine whether the bullet is in the chamber about to be fired or not.

People seem to be more willing to accept responsibility for good deeds than for bad deeds, for successes rather than failures, and for outcomes resulting from the actions of several people jointly rather than for outcomes produced by oneself alone. Since suicide is seen as morally wrong by most major religions, some potential suicides may see the participation of others, especially physicians, as making them less morally at fault themselves. As I mentioned in Chapter 7, one major theme found in suicide notes is justification by suicidal individuals for their presumed violation of the sacred trust of life. Thus, suicide notes often ask God for forgiveness and request significant others to pray for the deceased.

SHOULD ASSISTED SUICIDE BE MADE LEGAL?

Assisted suicide is no longer a hypothetical possibility—it is a reality. Not surprisingly, it has been discovered that American physicians have been assisting patients to die for many years without publicity. The core question is changing from "Should we permit assisted suicide?" to "Should we regulate assisted suicide?" There is much to be said for permitting and regulating a behavior instead of pretending that the behavior does not occur when in fact it does.

It has been claimed that psychologists and psychiatrists have too often supported the social *status quo* rather than agitating for change based on their understanding of human behavior. From this perspective, it is good that physicians who have been assisting suicide in the past without publicity have come forward to inform us that this practice has been occurring whether society approves or not and whether society regulates it or not.

Legalization of controversial actions can have advantages for a society. Only if actions are legalized can they be monitored closely and abuses corrected and avoided in the future. This has been the rationale in the Netherlands for legalizing many behaviors, including abortion, marijuana use, and assisted suicide.

In the United States there has been significant support for *banning* or making illegal such actions such as assisted suicide, gambling, prostitution, abortion, and recreational drug use. Prohibition leads to two consequences:

1. It drives the actions "underground." This results in an absence of supervision of the process, and it permits criminal elements to take over.

2. The people involved in these acts cannot be protected. Women die from "back-street" abortions, prostitutes are raped and sometimes murdered, and drug-users contract AIDS and other diseases from dirty needles.

Legalization of socially controversial acts means that people can be protected, even helped, and the process can be monitored and improved. And, make no mistake about it, the rich and the knowledgeable have always been able to engage in these behaviors. Before *Roe v. Wade* made abortion more easily obtainable, affluent Americans could get abortions easily. Armed with the right information, they could go to a private clinic in the Caribbean, have a "D&C," and come back with a sun tan after a week on the beach.

Even as far back as 1939, a celebrity like Sigmund Freud could find a physician to inject him with morphine. Criminalizing a behavior, such as assisted suicide, means among other things that the rest of us, those of us who aren't rich and famous, cannot engage in it or must do so illegally.

WHAT IF YOU ARE ASKED TO ASSIST IN SOMEONE'S SUICIDE?

Aside from helping to procure the means for suicide, you may be asked to assist someone in their suicide. Perhaps they simply want your presence, to hold their hand, as they die; perhaps they want you to mix the medication in some food that they will then eat themselves; or perhaps they want you to be more active—to actually pull the trigger of a gun?

Your presence is not against the law, although you may be required to report the death to the authorities. The more active you are in causing the death, however, the greater the possibility that you may be subject to a criminal charge. Therefore, until the laws are changed, it is wise to exercise the utmost discretion.

In his book *Final Exit,* Derek Humphry provided three criteria for helping you to decide whether to help a suicidal person:

1. Given your personal philosophy or set of moral values and given your relationship to the person, is this the right thing for *you* to do? Just as I have argued that suicidal people have the responsibility and the right to make their own choices, so do you in this situation. You do not have to allow yourself to be coerced into doing something you do not want to do, even if you believe in the idea.

2. Who else might know about the assisted suicide and will they keep it a secret if you ask them to? On the other hand, who else might help you and support you if you decide to help the suicidal person?

3. If a local law enforcement officer decides to charge you with a criminal act, and should your help become public knowledge, are you prepared to deal with the consequences?

In addition, I would suggest that you should try to find someone, a friend or a counselor, whom you can trust and to whom you can talk freely, so that you can sort out your feelings and thoughts about helping another commit suicide, both before and after you provide this assistance.

This book is concerned with making good decisions—informed, well thought-out, and discussed thoroughly with others. This goal is as relevant to the decision to help others commit suicide as it is in making the decision to kill yourself.

CHAPTER 9

What About The Law?

Although many people think that suicide is illegal in the United States, this is not true.

In a few states (Oklahoma, Texas, Washington, and Wisconsin), attempted suicide used to be a criminal act (and may still be). In some states, people who attempt suicide can be charged with an offense such as creating a public health hazard or a nuisance. After all, someone who jumps off a building, fires a gun, or leaves a car running may pose a danger to others who are in the vicinity or passing by. However, local authorities typically use the threat of charging those who make an attempt at suicide only to force them to seek professional help from a psychotherapist or psychiatrist. In most cases, people do not go to jail for attempting suicide, and those who succeed in killing themselves cannot be punished anyway.

It is not illegal to kill yourself in most developed countries of the world. In some countries where it used to be against the law, suicide has been decriminalized in recent years: New Zealand in 1961, Canada in 1972, and even Ireland in 1993.

However, assisting someone to commit suicide is a very different matter. The majority of American states and most other countries expressly forbid assisting suicide and make it a criminal offense to do so. Thus, assisting someone to kill himself is not a matter to be entered into lightly.

In June 1997, the United States Supreme Court ruled that the federal government could not interfere with state laws concerning assisted suicide, at least at the present time. The ruling permitted each state to decide whether or not to make assisting suicide a criminal offense. However, it is very likely that as states enact new legislation about assisted suicide, the Supreme Court will review more cases in this area.

Some states permit the use of force to prevent a person from committing suicide, and some states make it a crime to know about a suicidal death but fail to notify the police.

It is useful to find out about the criminal and civil statutes on suicide in your state. This information will help you safeguard yourself and your friends and family from unexpected legal action. The Hemlock Society has information that is useful here (www.hemlock.org).

SUICIDE AND LIFE INSURANCE

Another common misconception is that life insurance policies are invalid if you commit suicide. This is not true. I surveyed 20 life insurance companies, both large and small, and all but one had a 2-year limit. People who commit suicide within two years of taking out the policy are not eligible to receive the benefits. One of the companies I surveyed had only a 1-year limit. However, if the person commits suicide soon after taking out a policy, the beneficiary is still entitled to receive the premiums already paid, sometimes with interest.

Incidentally, it is not easy for insurance companies to prove suicide in court. Attorneys for the insurance companies are required to produce irrefutable evidence that the person died by his own hand (rather than accidentally, for example), and it is very hard to prove that the deceased had suicidal intent without a suicide note or clear verbal communication of suicidal intent before the death.

It would be useful, therefore, to check the terms of your insurance policy in order to ascertain how your company handles death by suicide, especially if you have only recently taken out the policy.

CHAPTER 10

If A Loved One Commits Suicide

Coping with the loss of a loved one can be painful, whether the loss is through divorce or death. Survivors experience intense, unpleasant emotions that can take months to dissipate. The death of a loved one is particularly difficult if the death is sudden, for a death without warning takes away any opportunity to finish incompleted tasks such as telling the person how much you loved him or her or restoring the relationship after friction and discord have crept into it.

Bereavement goes through a predictable course beginning with shock, numbness, and disbelief. The bereaved individual cannot believe that the person is dead. They can't seem to take in this information. Next there comes a yearning or pining for the deceased person and a feeling that you have been pushed into unfamiliar territory. In this stage, the rituals help. The funeral arrangements and ceremony serves to structure the time, and grief also provides relief in a way for it guides you in how you must behave. However, in this second stage, there may also be anger (at the deceased or at God for not preventing the death) and guilt (for not doing more to keep the person alive). There are "Why" and "What if . . . ?" questions.

The third stage is one of apathy and aimlessness. Life seems to have no structure, and there are no rules or guidelines for the bereaved until the fourth and final stage develops in which the bereaved person structures a new life without the lost loved one.

These days, there are many support groups for the bereaved, many books written with the aim of helping those who are bereaved, and a large amount of scholarly research and writing on bereavement.[1]

Yet, 50 years ago and for time immemorial before that, significant others died, and the survivors went through bereavement without professional help. Why do we need help with bereavement today? It is important to remember that life expectancy was quite short in the past. Living to the age of 50 was an achievement. Child mortality was high, and most parents lost many of their children to death. In addition, many generations of families lived in the same house (or at least the same village), and so children grew up experiencing the death of great-grandparents, grandparents, and parents as well as siblings. Bodies were laid out at home, and families members prepared the bodies for burial.

In contrast, today, homes with many generations of the same family living together are rare (geographic mobility means that the different generations may be separated by hundreds or thousands of miles), life expectancy is over 70 and creeping toward 80, and we have moved the task of burying the deceased out of the home into the funeral home. As a result, we have much less experience with death than our ancestors had in the past. Death is much more of a shock to us.

In the case of suicide, mourning is made worse for many reasons:

1. Since suicides rarely discuss their impending actions with their loved ones, suicidal deaths are sudden and unexpected, factors that make adjusting to the loss more difficult.

2. Some suicidal deaths are violent and leave the body in a particularly bloody state. Many of those who have written about surviving the suicide of a loved one have commented upon the trauma of finding the body, a shock that may have a lingering effect on the survivors for a lifetime.

3. Suicidal deaths often leave the survivors with feelings of guilt that are stronger than in the case of other causes of death. When people die suddenly, we may regret omissions such as apologizing for hurts we had caused or not telling them how much we loved them.

---

[1] Two scholarly journals, *Death Studies* and *Omega,* publish a large number of articles each year on bereavement.

But in cases of suicidal death, we may also feel guilt over failing to realize that they were in a desperate state and that we should have intervened in some way. A friend of mine whose colleague committed suicide asked himself why the colleague had not turned to him for help. He would, he told me, have done anything to help him—even taken him away to the Caribbean for a break. But his colleague did not turn to him for help, and that seemed to say that their friendship was not as close as he thought.

4. Suicidal deaths usually take place in family and friendship networks that are stressed and in conflict. If their relationships were healthy and supportive, suicidal individuals might not be considering ending their lives. The stress and conflict in these networks make resolution of the grief more difficult not only because the survivors fear that the stress and conflict may have contributed to the suicide, but also because they cannot turn to one another for comfort and support due to the conflicts that still remain in the family network.

5. Sometimes individuals who die by suicide are not given the same funeral ceremonies as those who died natural deaths. Ministers and priests may insist on different services and burial arrangements, and the mourning ritual may be changed. These departures from the normal customs increase feelings of uneasiness in the survivors. For example, friends may be inhibited in their response to the survivors in the case of suicide, feeling that they do not know what to say.

6. Suicidal deaths sometimes create feelings of blame and anger both within the family (Why didn't I sit down and talk to him?) and among the friends (Why didn't the family members take him for counseling when they saw how depressed he was?). As a result, the survivors may become alienated from one another and provide less support to each other during this difficult time.

An example of the reactions of the "community" to a suicidal death can be found in the case of the American poet Sylvia Plath, who committed suicide in London in 1963 by inhaling fumes from a gas oven. (In those days, many English homes used coal gas, which was very toxic because of its high carbon monoxide content.) Sylvia was living in an apartment with her two children after her husband, the British poet Ted Hughes, had left her for another woman. Some feminists have since held Ted responsible for driving Sylvia to suicide. In fact, every time a grave marker was placed on Sylvia's grave, her married name was effaced. One feminist writer has even accused

Hughes of murder. Unfortunately for Ted, the woman for whom he left Sylvia also committed suicide. Even I used to say in talks that Ted was a dangerous person, having driven two women to suicide.

This is really quite unfair. Sylvia had been continually depressed throughout her life. She made a very serious attempt to kill herself when she was 21, after which she stayed in a psychiatric clinic and was given electroconvulsive therapy in order to try to alleviate her depression. A psychiatric colleague of mine once offered his opinion that Sylvia probably had a manic-depressive disorder and that today she might have been helped with lithium, a medication that has improved life for many people suffering with a bipolar affective disorder.

It is certainly true that, if everyone who experienced the break-up of a marriage or long-term relationship committed suicide, the country would be severely depopulated. Four of the eight colleagues with whom I work have been divorced; I have been divorced twice, in addition to having had four romantic relationships end—and we are all still alive. Having a spouse or a lover leave is neither necessary nor sufficient for suicide. This is not to deny the fact that Sylvia Plath experienced psychological suffering so unbearable for her that she killed herself. But Ted Hughes was no more to blame than any other spouse who falls out of love and leaves home. Still a tendency to "blame the other" often arises in cases of suicide.

7. There may also be a feeling of rejection. Suicides reject their loved ones by removing themselves without discussing it with those left behind. A suicide is similar in this respect to a spouse who deserts his or her partner.

8. When someone dies from cancer, for example, the bereaved are clear about the causes of the death. When someone dies from suicide, however, the "Why?" questions persist and are more complicated. We scholars and clinicians who study and counsel suicidal individuals often feel that we have no meaningful or satisfactory explanation of why some particular individual committed suicide, and yet we have the benefit of being up-to-date in our knowledge about suicidal behavior. Ordinary people are, therefore, even more puzzled by the suicide of their loved one. It is very hard for the bereaved to accept that they will never fully understand why their loved one chose to commit suicide.

The lack of social support and the scarcity of friends who understand what survivors of suicide experience has led to the growth of survivor groups for those who lose a loved one to suicide[2] and to the publication of many books for survivors to read, such as *Silent Grief* by Christopher Lucas and Henry Seiden or *A Special Scar* by Alison Wertheimer. There are also support groups for those bereaved as a result of loved ones dying from any cause.

The difficulty of bereavement after suicide is why, in this book, I urge people who are thinking about and planning suicide to discuss their thoughts and feelings with their loved ones and, if possible, to go to a counselor who could contribute to these discussions. If they are open and sincere, such communications can go far in easing the grief of survivors.[3]

---

[2] The American Association of Suicidology publishes a directory of survivor groups in the United States (Suite 408, 4201 Connecticut Avenue NW, Washington, DC 20008. 202-237-2280), Web site www.suicidology.org.

[3] If assisting suicide is legalized in some form in some states in America, this "decriminalization" will help to remove some of the stigma of suicide and the negative moral judgments that some people make about the act.

CHAPTER 11

Preparing For Death:
Some Simple Tasks

Before a person commits suicide, indeed before any of us dies from whatever cause, there are tasks and issues that must be considered.

WILLS AND SUICIDE NOTES

We all need to have a will that lists in detail what we own and to whom do we want to leave it. Some people often leave instructions in their suicide note in place of a will. Give this to Bill; pay Joan the money I owe her. Still, it is wiser to have made a formal will. It is also advisable for you to settle as many of your affairs as possible before you die, whether of natural causes or by your own hand.

If you do decide to kill yourself, whether your loved ones are involved with the decision or not, it is useful to leave a suicide note, both to help your loved ones adjust to your death and to spare them any legal entanglements caused by your suicide.

If you haven't shared your decision with anyone else, it is helpful to your survivors to have some information about your circumstances and why you have decided to kill yourself. Survivors report that they continually wonder why a loved one committed suicide, and this unanswerable question often dominates their thoughts for years afterwards.

Even if you have shared your decision with others, and perhaps made the decision after consulting with them, a suicide note is still a practical means of preventing your loved ones from encountering legal difficulties. It is useful to state that you are of sound mind, just as in a will, to explain why you are committing suicide, and to stress that you are solely responsible for the decision and that nobody persuaded you or forced you to commit suicide. This will protect your family from criminal charges.

ADVANCE MEDICAL DIRECTIVES

We need to communicate our opinions and desires about the medical care we want before we are no longer capable of conveying this to others. Advance medical directives are a set of instructions about our desires in this area.

A "living will" or a "directive to physicians" may state that you desire to be allowed to die a natural death without the use of extraordinary medical treatment, heroic measures, or artificial means that will not improve your health, but simply maintain your life. Alternatively it may state that you do want to be kept alive. Although a living will should be witnessed, you should understand that it is a request, not an order, and it cannot be legally enforced.

A "durable power of attorney" is a legal document in which you designate someone else to make medical decisions on your behalf when you are physically and mentally unable to do so yourself. The "attorney-in-fact" does not have to be a lawyer, but can be anybody you choose for the task. A durable power of attorney can be legally enforced.

The American Association of Retired Persons has a booklet on advance directives that can be obtained by writing to

AARP
601 E Street NW
Washington, DC 20049
800 424 3410
www.aarp.org

Advance directive forms (including living wills and medical power of attorney) can be obtained from

Partnerships For Caring
Suite 202
1620 Eye Street NW
Washington, DC 20006
202 296 8071
www.partnershipsforcaring.org

A values history form, which offers a framework for thinking about and deciding these issues, can be obtained from

Center for Health Law and Ethics
Institute of Public Law
University of New Mexico School of Law
1117 Stanford NE
Albuquerque, NM 87131
www.ipl.unm.edu/chle/

It is useful to inform your family and physician that you have such documents and to make sure that a trusted person has updated copies or knows where they are stored. All of these documents should be notarized to be effective.

It is important to make several copies of living wills and powers of attorney. Give copies to your significant others, to your physician (or physicians), and to the hospitals involved in your care. Have copies with you when you are admitted to the hospital, just in case your documents have been mislaid or misfiled. If these documents are not available at the right time and place, they are not going to help you.

It is important to talk about the issues in your living will with your doctors. Ask them such questions as what their views are on engaging in heroic measures to keep people alive, whether they are prepared to give sufficient pain medication, and even whether they would prescribe a lethal dose of a medication for you under certain circumstances.

You might also want to contact the Hemlock Society or Compassion In Dying, national organizations concerned with the dignity of dying and death, to obtain their booklets, ask specific questions, or obtain free counseling.

The Hemlock Society USA
P O Box 101810
Denver, CO 80250-1810
800 247 7421
www.hemlock.org

Compassion In Dying
415
6312 SW Capitol Highway
Portland, OR 97201
503 221 9556
www.compassionindying.org

ERGO: Euthanasia Research & Guidance Organization
(World Federation of Right to Die Societies)
www.finalexit.org

FUNERAL ARRANGEMENTS

In most cases, people do not make arrangements for their own funerals. After their death, their grieving loved ones are left to make these arrangements at a time and in a state when it is very difficult to make rational decisions. A sudden death from whatever cause makes arranging a funeral even more difficult for the survivors. Research indicates that people who arrange a funeral for someone who died suddenly may spend more for the funeral than they do for someone whose dying took place over a longer period of time.

The rituals of the funeral can be therapeutic for the bereaved, but arranging the funeral can be made easier for the bereaved if some thought was given to the funeral months or years in advance.

You *can* make arrangements for your own funeral before you die. You can choose the form of funeral you want, whether you want to be buried or cremated, and even pre-pay for it. To do this would spare your loved ones a great deal of anguish, and it ensures that your funeral is consistent with your values and lifestyle.

Even if you do not go this far, have you discussed what you want done with your body after death? Do you prefer cremation or burial? Do you wish to have a religious ceremony, a secular ceremony, or no ceremony at all? Do you want to donate your organs to others or your body to scientific research? Have you filled out a donor card, and do your loved ones know your intentions?

In short, the more thorough you are in arranging your affairs before the suicide, the easier it will be for your family to cope with your death. Your efforts will not only convey to your loved ones your determination to end your life, but it will also show how much you still care for them.

The Decision to Die

CHAPTER 12

Making The Psychological Decision Whether Or Not To Commit Suicide

There are many *systems* of psychotherapy and counseling—that is, guides for psychotherapists to follow in counseling clients. The system provides a theory of the causes of psychological distress, goals for the psychotherapist to aim for, and techniques for the psychotherapist to follow.

There is one system of psychotherapy, *Direct Decision Therapy,* that is not found in any of the textbooks I use in the college courses that I teach, yet I think that it is one of the most important systems of psychotherapy and should be studied by every psychotherapist. It is the only system of therapy that deals with decision-making— and committing suicide involves making a very important decision. Indeed, since we make decisions every moment of our lives, improving our decision-making skills would be of great value to us in dealing with any of the problems that we face during our lives.

Before I discuss this system of psychotherapy, consider the following situation. Pretend that you are going for your first visit to a psychotherapist tomorrow. You know that the therapist will ask you, "What is your problem? Why have you come to see me?" How would you respond? Write your answer on this page.

Direct Decision Therapy, a system proposed by Harold Greenwald, focuses upon the decisions that people make. The task of the psychotherapist is to help clients; 1) find out about the decisions they have made in the past that have led to their current problems; 2) make decisions to change their behavior; and 3) carry out these new decisions. The basic assumption made by the system is that the problem you wrote down on the previous page is the result of a decision or decisions you have made.

The first question asked of a client who enters therapy is "What's your problem?" Specific situational problems are easier to focus on. To answer "I have an unhappy marriage" or "I am afraid of heights" sets out a clear problem to deal with. A personality or lifestyle problem is less specific. For example, saying "I am unhappy" or "I am passive" expresses a way of being and of living. Greenwald sees all such problems as decisions that the client made. *People choose to be unhappy or passive.* The psychotherapist has to help the client search for the decisions made in the past that initiated this state of mind, in essence this lifestyle.

Greenwald also emphasizes the importance of finding out about the context in which former decisions were made. Once the context is found, the decision will appear to be appropriate given the context. After this, the psychotherapist can assist clients in deciding whether they want to change.

Greenwald described a psychiatric patient that he interviewed in front of the staff of a mental hospital in order to demonstrate *Direct Decision Therapy.* Marie was a typical, hopeless schizophrenic. After she had entered the room and screamed incoherently, she calmed down and Greenwald asked her how he could help her. She told him that she wanted to get out of "this crazy place." Greenwald told her that he could help her, but first he asked her when she decided to act crazy? She replied:

> That's an easy question. . . . When I was five years old I was having an argument with my mother and she said, "You're crazy," and I thought to myself, if you think I'm crazy now, I'll show you what crazy is. And after that I was terrible (Greenwald, 1978, p. 32).

I could ask hundreds of schizophrenics the same question and not get a similar answer. But Marie's case, though unusual, does serve to illustrate Greenwald's point that we do make decisions about such matters. I have also been able to identify personal experiences that fitted with Greenwald's theory.

After I had emigrated to the United States in 1964, I began to monitor the letters my mother and I wrote to each other back and forth across the Atlantic Ocean. If I wrote cheerful and newsy letters, she wrote sad and depressed responses. On the other hand, if I was sad and depressed and told her about this, she wrote back cheery letters. Since I was chronically depressed at the time, I began to wonder if I had "decided" to be depressed.

My parents had an unhappy marriage, and my father left home when I was 12. My mother was very depressed (and remained so for the rest of her life), and she also became phobic. She could not go shopping or travel on buses and trains unless I was with her. It was as if my mother, having lost her husband, unconsciously wanted to make sure that she did not lose her son. So, unless I was at school, I had to be with her all the time. I remember that she was very caring when I was ill; she would nurse me devotedly. I used to have a little bell in the shape of a lady with a gown beside my bed, which I could ring if I needed her. After my mother's death, this was one of the items I brought back to the United States.

I do not remember "deciding" to be depressed in order to get my mother's attention and care. But it seems likely that, as a 12-year-old, I noticed how my mother took care of me when I was ill or depressed; so I probably "decided," consciously or unconsciously, that this was a good tactic on my part when I wanted her attention.

It's not a bad tactic for a 12 year old; after all, 12-year-olds are not well versed in interpersonal dynamics and don't have as many interpersonal skills as they will have in later years. As Greenwald notes, once you identify the context in which the decision was made, it will probably appear to be quite rational. But a good tactic for a 12 year old is not necessarily a good tactic for a 30 year old. Maybe I needed to change the decision to be more depressed than my mother as we exchanged letters when I was in my 20s.[1]

After identifying the decisions people have made that have resulted in their "problems," the next step is to help clients decide whether they want to change. In pursuit of this goal, it is useful to focus on the payoffs of various decisions. Both the positive gain and

---

[1] It also occurred to me that I might be relating to my friends and lovers in the same way, presenting myself as a depressed person so that they would take care of me. I decided to look for and eliminate any tendencies in myself along these lines.

the negative gain from the decisions that have been made must be examined, and this must be done without criticizing the client.

The client must be confronted with the question, "Would you like to change?" However, Greenwald opposes forcing clients to change. He argues that it is not for the psychotherapist to decide this, but for the client. One way to help clients to decide is to help them find alternatives. Often they are unable to think of any spontaneously, but with the psychotherapist's encouragement, they eventually can. It is important that the clients do most of this work themselves for Greenwald wants people to learn a system that they can apply by themselves to problems encountered in the future. So it is imperative that clients take an active role in their psychotherapy.

Once clients have found an alternative, they must be encouraged to look at the payoffs once again. These payoffs and consequences must be compared with the payoffs of the previous decision. Greenwald is content to have clients stop here. He wants clients simply to be aware of their choices. They do not have to change. However, if they do decide to change, the psychotherapist can help them carry the decision through. The psychotherapist also has to make sure that clients realize that a decision must be reaffirmed constantly and that one lapse does not mean that they have to abandon their new decision.

Greenwald is quite willing to use techniques from other systems of psychotherapy that are consistent with his orientation. For example, role playing can be useful; Greenwald sometimes suggests that clients act the way they would like to be. He will set homework exercises for his clients to complete, and he uses the client's behavior in psychotherapy for practice in decision-making. If a client comes late to a psychotherapy session, Greenwald may say "Come on time, or as late as you like. It's your money." Not only is this a ploy that gets the client to come on time, but it also is true. It is the client's choice. Greenwald has clients decide how long they want to be in psychotherapy and will let clients choose the technique, what to focus on in the discussion, and even whether to lie on a couch or not. All these situations give clients practice in making decisions.

Direct Decision Therapy can be brief, especially if the basic decisions are easy to identify. For example, a client may come with a problem of whether or not to go out with a specific man. Discussion with the psychotherapist may reveal that the basic decision she has made is to go out only with those men who make her suffer so that she can justify a belief that all men are no good.

A central principle in *Direct Decision Therapy* is not to impose values on the client. Its main principle is that clients should be free to choose whatever they want. As Greenwald phrased it himself:

> My real goal is awareness, an awareness in terms of the choice he has made, the context in which he made the choice, and the payoffs (Greenwald, 1973, p. 151).

DECIDING ABOUT SUICIDE

In deciding about suicide it is important to follow the same steps as Greenwald has described in *Direct Decision Therapy.* Six steps can be identified, and each will be discussed in detail.

First

What are your current problems? If you were to go to a psychotherapist today, what would you present as your problems? Are you depressed, lonely, an alcoholic, or in pain? If so, could you have decided, at least in part, to be this?

Obviously, people don't choose to have cancer or Alzheimer's disease. And there are those who prefer to believe that we somehow inherited many of the problems and that they are biochemically or neurophysiologically caused. Don't blame me—blame my genes. Every week, newspapers and magazines tell us that conditions such as homosexuality, obesity, and the desire to take risks are caused by our genes and that "scientists" will soon unlock the secrets to the "problem" and find a way to change us using genetic engineering. Maybe so.

Or maybe not. It still might be useful for you to consider that you decided to be depressed (as I did), or that you decided to be lonely or to be an alcoholic. In the process of searching for the decision and the context, you can learn something about yourself, and you will begin to prepare yourself for future decisions too.

Second

If the answer might be "yes" to the question of whether you made such decisions, then ask yourself when did you decide this, in what circumstances did you decide this, and do you still think that you should abide by the same decision? Of course, to explore this fully, you would benefit from having a Direct Decision psychotherapist to talk to. And most likely you will not find one because few exist. However, if you are assertive, you might ask your psychotherapist to read Greenwald's book and help you identify the sources of your decisions so that some of them could be changed.

But among the reasons I wrote this book was to offer help to those of you who have to face all of this by yourself.

Third

Although the majority of people have thought about committing suicide at some point in their lives, what are your thoughts about *suicide right now*? Have you found yourself thinking that suicide might be an option for you now? What were the circumstances in which you began to think about suicide as a serious option?

My mother died from cancer, and so cancer seems like an appropriate choice for me to use as an example. Perhaps I am considering suicide because I have cancer and only a 20 percent chance of surviving for one year, according to the best medical estimates. What is it about this situation that leads me to consider suicide?

Is it the pain?

Is it the limitations on my lifestyle (for example, having to be confined to bed)?

Is it the financial burden on my family?

Is it the fear of being a nuisance to them when they have to take care of me, especially if I begin to soil the bed and need someone to feed me?

Is it the uncertainty of what is next?

Is it the perception of the slow deterioration of my life?

Is it the fear of life after death?

Each of us will list different factors, perhaps some of the above, plus other aspects that did not occur to me for this situation.

Fourth

Now take each of these factors in turn. Suicide is clearly one solution for some of the aspects listed above. What are other possible solutions? For example, take the interpersonal burden—that others have to disrupt their lives to take care of us and that they have to perform possibly disgusting and annoying chores in order to keep us alive. Are there any other options?

Perhaps there are friends and relatives who could tolerate these chores better than others. After all, our closest relatives (husband, wife, child, or parent) may be least able to do so, whereas a cousin or an aunt may find it easier to cope. Perhaps these helpers could share the tasks and, therefore, the burden.

Perhaps there is enough money to pay for a nurse or a home health care aide to come in from time to time to perform some of these chores.

Perhaps it would make sense for us to enter a hospital, a nursing home, or a hospice.

Perhaps, rather than finding a hospice to live in until we die, we could arrange for home hospice care.

Each of these options has advantages and disadvantages—both for us and for our relatives. For example, perhaps we dread being in a nursing home, but our relatives would prefer that option. On the other hand, perhaps we would prefer being in a nursing home, but our relatives would feel too guilty if they agreed to that idea.

For each aspect of our current situation, we need to lay out the options and to list the advantages and disadvantages of each. And we need to do this, not simply by ourselves, but with the others involved in our lives—our spouses, children, parents, distant relatives, and friends.

Keeping careful notes is a good idea. Maintain a notebook in which you write out the problems and break them into aspects. For each aspect list all the known alternatives (including suicide), and note the advantages and disadvantages of each alternative.

Fifth

Let us assume that after consideration of all of these alternatives, with their advantages and disadvantages, you still think that you want to commit suicide. First, ask yourself what are the advantages of this choice? Then list them in your notebook, together with the disadvantages. What is the best alternative to suicide? What are the advantages and disadvantages of this alternative? Again write them down in your notebook. Then weigh the two alternatives. Which do you choose?

Sixth

Let us assume that you have chosen suicide. Now you have a series of tasks to complete. First of all, how would you prefer to kill yourself?

In *Final Exit,* Derek Humphry helps people choose a method for suicide. He prefers the use of medications combined with a plastic bag placed over the head, and he gives the sizes of drug overdoses that will be fatal for a number of common medications. However, that is *his* choice.

In my research I have asked many people about their preferred method for suicide, and their responses cover a range of methods. Just as firearms are the most popular method among the roughly 30,000 Americans who commit suicide each year (the most popular method now both for men and for women), many of the people I have questioned choose firearms too.

But you must decide on *your* preferred method.

Next you have to procure the necessary materials for your method of choice. It may take a while to obtain the needed medications or to purchase a firearm, and there are procedures to follow, such as applying for a permit to purchase a gun, or finding an appropriate reason to give to physicians in order for them to agree to prescribe a lethal medication. Remember that, despite all of the current debate about physician-assisted suicide, most physicians will not prescribe a lethal medication if you are honest about your suicidal intent. Remember also that in some countries, lethal medications are available without a prescription. The Hemlock Society (www.hemlock.org) can provide some advice for obtaining the means to commit suicide.

A factor to consider at this point is that you probably have family, relatives, and friends who should be involved in your decision. In the next chapter, I will discuss the advantages of getting them involved in your decision, perhaps with the help of a counselor. Your suicide will affect them greatly, and unless you are very angry at them and want to hurt them, all of you will feel better if the decision is discussed by everyone beforehand.

DECISIONS ARE NOT FINAL

It is important to remember that your decisions are not necessarily final. You can change your mind, and it is perfectly all right to do so.

For instance, say you are very ill with cancer. You may decide to try chemotherapy for your cancer, but after several weeks of treatment, you may change your mind and decide to let the cancer take its course and to commit suicide as the pain increases. That is fine. Or you may decide to commit suicide, but after a few days, decide instead to try chemotherapy. That is fine too.

Of course, since death is involved, at some point you reach a final decision. But up to that point, changes of mind are entirely acceptable.

CHAPTER 13

Getting The Family Involved

Having a loved one commit suicide is, of course, extremely traumatic. Research evidence indicates that the relatives and friends of suicides, people whom we refer to as *survivors,* experience greater guilt, receive less social support, and feel more of a need to understand why the death occurred than those who experience the natural death of a loved one. There is a whole range of emotions, thoughts, behaviors, interpersonal reactions, and physical symptoms that survivors can experience.

The emotions experienced include grief, anger, and depression; the thoughts include shock, disbelief, and denial; the behaviors include sleep disturbances and, sometimes, increased smoking and drinking; the interpersonal reactions include changes in social contacts and the type of communication; and the physical symptoms include illness and mortality. David Brent and his colleagues found evidence for significant psychopathology, especially depression and post-traumatic stress disorder symptoms, as much as six months after the suicide of a friend or acquaintance.

A suicidal death is traumatic for the survivors partly because it is often unexpected and sudden. Although the suicidal person may have given cues to the impending event, some suicides do not give cues, while in other cases the family and friends do not recognize these cues accurately. The suddenness of the death leaves the survivors with unfinished business—questions that are left unanswered, issues and conflicts that are unresolved, and expressions of love and affection that went unspoken.

Furthermore, in many cases survivors are traumatized by being the ones who discovered the body. The suicide may even take place in the presence of significant others. In some cases, there is great hostility on the part of the suicide, and the act of suicide serves to satisfy both a wish to die and a desire to punish family members or close friends by forcing them to witness the trauma of the death, creating an extremely unpleasant memory for the survivor. The following is a typical case:

> A 28-year-old female who had been sexually abused as a child and who suffered from chronic low self-esteem, was having marital and financial problems (she quit paying the household bills and did not tell her husband). She called her husband at work one day and asked him to come home for lunch, telling him that she had a surprise for him. As he entered the house, she walked up to him and shot herself in the head with a .38 pistol (McDowell et al., 1994, p. 218).

In other cases, the witness to the suicide may be a friend or acquaintance who is less involved in the dynamics of the suicide:

> A 22-year-old male with a history of alcohol abuse and marital problems was depressed over a recent breakup with his girl-friend. . . . As he was riding with a friend another individual's car, they were discussing his problems. He asked his friend to give him his gun. When the friend handed a .32 pistol to him, he calmly put it to his head and shot himself (McDowell et al., 1994, p. 219).

Even if the suicidal act itself is not witnessed, the body of the suicide is often discovered by those closest to the deceased, who then are left with a very unpleasant and horrifying visual memory of their loved one.

Some suicides feel alienated from their family and friends; indeed they may be very angry at them. For these people, the thought of hurting these significant others may be part of the motivation for committing suicide. Persons in this frame of mind will not care about the concerns of this chapter. They will not want their significant others to be in any way involved with their plans, and that is their decision.

Often survivors of suicides can benefit from counseling. There is an active group of survivors in the American Association of

Suicidology, and groups of survivors across America can meet regularly if they wish for support and counseling.[1] In addition, many families choose to go into counseling after a loved one commits suicide, and those who do not sometimes regret not doing so. One of the latter, Susan White-Bowden, wrote a book about her experiences. She divorced her husband, but he refused to accept the finality of the divorce. He came to her house one evening, and tried to persuade Susan to continue their marriage. When she refused, he went upstairs and shot himself. Susan had three children, two daughters and a son, Jody, aged 14. Susan did not share her feelings with the children after this trauma, nor did she consider counseling for the family. She tried to act as if everything was fine—she referred to herself as a "Susie Sunshine." By the age of 17, Jody had shown some behavioral problems (vandalism at school and driving while high on marijuana). After his girlfriend broke up with him and refused to get back together, Jody went home and shot himself. In retrospect, Susan realized that she should have taken the family for counseling after her husband's suicide.

Some suicidal people kill themselves after a long period of deliberation, accompanied by a cumulative succession of material or personal losses, chronic depression, alcohol abuse, or medical illness. Their significant others may be aware of this process and yet are at a loss to know what to do. It is not easy living with people who have chronic problems, and their relatives and friends would benefit from support and counseling for themselves.

---

[1] For help with bereavement in Great Britain after the death of a loved one from any kind of cause, the Cruse Organization provides help:

Cruse House
126 Sheen Road
Richmond
Surrey TW9 1UR
UK
www.crusebereavementcare.org.uk

In Canada, the Canadian Mental Health Association can provide help:

CMHA National Office
3rd Floor
2160 Yonge Street
Toronto, Ontario M4S 2Z3
Canada
www.cmha.ca

IF SUICIDE HURTS SURVIVORS, SHOULD
WE NOT KILL OURSELVES?

Some people draw the implication that we should not commit suicide because it brings suffering to others. Does this conclusion make sense? I think that the answer is no.

A British bishop once declared that he would die content that he had made at least one person in the world happy—the woman he did not marry! As I mentioned in Chapter 7, compared to suicide, a much greater case might be made against letting people get married or have children. Far more spouses do great harm to their mates, and parents to their children, than the few suicides do to their kin. Yet we do not forbid marriages or prevent people from having children. On the contrary, we counsel those who have been divorced as well as those who come from dysfunctional families. Although we need to provide counseling for suicide survivors who request it, their trauma does not make suicide immoral, irrational, or inappropriate for the suicidal person.

Indeed, if we were to reorient our approach to suicidal people, it would be possible to provide counseling for a family in which one member has decided to commit suicide. The family as a group could come to share, participate in, understand, and accept the decision of the suicidal member. For example, Betty Rollin helped her mother, who was dying of cancer and who refused to have further chemotherapy, to commit suicide. Betty and her husband could have been helped by a counselor, had one been available, so that they could have explored and worked through the myriad of feelings they had to contend with as they prepared for the mother's suicide.

More and more in recent years, suicidal people are seeking assisted suicide. Since physicians can provide the preferred means for suicide, in the form of painless medications, some suicidal individuals consider asking a physician to provide the drugs with which to commit suicide or even to administer them by injection—what we now call *physician-assisted suicide*. Yet the decisions made by these individuals are often opposed by loved ones, and the problems of obtaining the medications and taking them in a way that ensures that there will be no legal consequences for the survivors can make the process very unpleasant. The suicide may be left alone to take the pills, the survivors are anxious, and the decision has been inadequately discussed by those involved.

When Betty Rollin decided to help her mother to commit suicide, she could find no assistance from physicians in the United States. A friend gave her the name of a physician in the Netherlands who told her how to arrange her mother's death. She obtained a prescription for Nembutal, supposedly for insomnia, and her mother took the tablets while Betty and her husband sat with her. In order to avoid being accused of causing her mother's death, Betty and her husband did not remain until the end. Her mother was found dead the next morning by the daytime maid.

THE ROLE OF
SIGNIFICANT OTHERS

During the process of deciding about suicide there is obviously a role for significant others. They too have desires, thoughts, and emotions that can be explored with the assistance of a counselor. The patterns of communication between the suicidal person and the significant others may be less than complete and honest because of the emotions involved. Each party may feel anger, anxiety, and depression in their attempts to talk to one another. Therefore, each member of the network can certainly benefit both from individual sessions with the counselor and from family therapy as a group.

In this way, when the decisions are made, each member of the family can feel that their opinion has been heard, that they have played an important role in the discussion, and that the decision has been appropriate. The surviving members of the family will still experience grief, and perhaps other emotions, after the suicide, but less intensely since some of these feelings will have been communicated and worked through prior to the death.

The suicidal death will not be a surprise to the survivors. The death can be arranged so that they will not have to deal with the body, and the process itself can be transformed from a traumatic and shocking event into a uniting and healing ceremony.

A good example of this process comes from the Netherlands, reported by a psychologist, René Diekstra. Mr. L had cancer and was given no more than six months to live. He was a retired civil servant, a stubborn man with a defeatist attitude toward life. His wife was informed of his prognosis first and communicated this to her husband, after which he declared that he wished to end his life with medications. He felt that his life was useless, and he feared dependence on physicians, burdening his wife with nursing, and the degeneration of his body.

One of his sons was a physician, but he refused to become involved with his father's decision. Mr. L's general practitioner refused to provide medications but said that he would withhold treatment if, for example, Mr. L caught pneumonia. The other family members did not object to Mr. L's suicide, but Mr. L's wife thought that it was too soon for him to die. Their relationship was still rewarding, and she saw that her husband could still enjoy some aspects of living, at least for a while. She did not want him to die in pain from the cancer, but she also feared that her husband might try to kill himself by other, more violent methods if he was not provided with medication, a situation that she would find traumatic.

At Diekstra's suggestion, Mr. L's wife told her husband that she thought it was too early for him to die and that she would miss him if he died at that moment. He was pleased to hear this and glad that he was still needed. He agreed to postpone the decision, but he wanted assurance that he would be given the medication when the appropriate time arrived. He was given this assurance, and he lived for two more months.

Diekstra noted that, apart from simply providing the man with the necessary medication for suicide, he acknowledged the acceptability of Mr. L's request and mobilized communication within the family, getting the wife and the children involved. Mr. L came to feel less anxious and agitated, and he was able to participate more constructively in the life of his family for his final two months of life. The process improved the quality of life for both Mr. L and his family.

Diekstra pointed out that "assisted suicide" means more than just providing the medications necessary for death. It should also involve providing technical information on means for committing suicide, removal of obstacles such as getting the person released from an institution, giving advice on precautions and actions (such as making a will), and remaining with the person until the very end. We might add that it should also involve the counseling of both the client and the significant others by a counselor who is sensitized to the issues involved.

CAN YOU FIND SUCH A COUNSELOR?

Because of both the scarcity of professionals who have the appropriate orientation and the legal climate at the present time, finding a counselor with concern and expertise in suicide counseling is not an easy task. This state of affairs led to two of the goals of this book. The first goal is a plea to counselors and psychotherapists that this is one role that they ought to consider accepting as part of their responsibilities as professionals. Counselors should realize, too, that the type of counseling required for the family of the potential suicide may differ substantially from that which would help suicidal people to make up their minds, for which individual face-to-face counseling is more suitable, at least initially.

As we have noted elsewhere in this book, the majority of counselors are made very uneasy by suicidal clients. Most counselors have very little experience with suicidal people, and, when inexperienced counselors encounter such clients, they become acutely anxious. Suicide is not a topic they feel comfortable discussing, and they will tend to avoid the topic or refer the client to another counselor. Quite often they are scared. What if they say the wrong thing and their client goes out and kills himself? This fear immobilizes them and makes them less competent as counselors.

There is also the possibility that having a suicidal client makes counselors contemplate their own existence. "If clients in their own situations find life so unbearable that they are thinking about committing suicide, why don't I consider it also? After all, my life is just as unbearable." Just as physicians often lose what few interpersonal skills they have when confronted with dying patients, because such patients force them to confront their own mortality, so too counselors would prefer not to work with clients who have given up on life.

In today's litigious society, counselors also fear lawsuits. If the client commits suicide, will the family sue the counselor? It shouldn't be surprising that many counselors are more concerned with protecting their livelihood than with helping their client. They may administer psychological tests that are useless for helping the client, but useful if the counselor is sued. A test score indicating that a client was not a high risk for suicide can be used by the counselor to fight a claim of negligence or malpractice. If the client is a high risk for suicide, some counselors may consider informing the relatives and getting the client hospitalized so that they can say in court, "But I did my best to prevent my client's suicide."

We are not going to change the proclivity of Americans to sue at the drop of a hat, and so it is unlikely that most counselors will become any more willing to take the needs of suicidal clients into account.

One solution to this difficulty is to find a counselor or psychotherapist who is a member of the American Association of Suicidology. My colleagues in the AAS who are counselors are experienced in working with suicidal clients. As a result they are less anxious and more skilled in their dealings with such clients. On the other hand, the majority of association members want to prevent suicide; they prefer not to encourage it. So they may be biased in favor of their clients continuing to live.[2]

Even the best counselors have their limitations. A couple of years ago, I was feeling quite depressed after two operations, and I was wishing that I had died when my heart had stopped beating for a minute. While attending a conference on suicide, I mentioned my suicidal thoughts to a colleague who happened to be a psychotherapist, but he ignored my communication. I attributed his avoidance of the topic to the fact that he was used to discussing suicidal impulses in his office, but with a friend outside of an office setting, his anxiety got the better of him—it was the wrong context for him to be a good counselor.

Another possibility is to find a counselor (perhaps a social worker or a psychologist) who has experience in hospice care, the care of dying people either in formal hospices or at home. These counselors do not become anxious in the face of death, and many of their clients become suicidal at some point during the dying process. As a consequence, these counselors are reasonably comfortable when discussing such thoughts and feelings with their clients. One of my students, a psychology major who obtained a graduate degree in social work, worked for a home hospice program in which dying clients remain at home and the services they need are delivered to them there. She has recently opened a private counseling practice. She would be an ideal counselor for suicidal persons and their families.

---

[2] The Hemlock Society (www.hemlock.org) and Compassion in Dying (www.compassionindying.org) can help in providing appropriate counseling.

THE DO-IT-YOURSELF SOLUTION

The second goal for this book is to help readers plan and carry out their suicide by themselves. If we can't turn to professionals for help in this process, then we are forced to do it by ourselves. Dying, obviously, is a process we only engage in once. Unfortunately, we don't get to practice dying. A guide to some of the problems and issues involved would be very helpful.

Hence this book—with chapters on each of the issues and steps involved so that you can follow them without a counselor.

And if you are lucky enough to find a good counselor, you may still use this book as a guide. You can take a copy to your counselor and say, "This is what I want to do. Please read it and tell me whether you are able to help me in the process."

A FINAL COMMENT

On July 6, 1997, Ann Landers ran four letters from survivors of suicides—three people whose fathers committed suicide and one whose son committed suicide. All tried to convince a previous writer not to kill herself. What was notable about the four writers was that all four of their loved ones committed suicide without warning, and one writer specifically noted that she came home from school to find her father's body.

There were no warnings.

They discovered the body.

The process I have described in this book ideally gets the family involved beforehand, thereby eliminating both the unexpectedness of the suicide and the shock of finding the body, a trauma that can linger on for the rest of a survivor's life. I sincerely hope that potential suicides, their families and friends, and mental health professionals will all find this book helpful.

CHAPTER 14

Planning Your Death Ceremony

It is my belief that we need to work to change society so that dying becomes a less frightening and more pleasant process. Some progress has already been made through establishment of hospices and the training of medical and mental health professionals to deal with dying patients more compassionately. There is no reason to exclude suicidal deaths from these considerations.

Alfred Nobel, founder of the Nobel Prizes, proposed many years ago that a luxurious villa should be built on the French Riviera overlooking the Mediterranean Sea where people could go in order to commit suicide in beautiful surroundings. Fanciful though Nobel's vision may be, it is the compassion in his vision that I would like to build upon. Following that spirit, we can create our own ceremony for our death, whether from suicide or other causes. We usually put a lot of thought and expense into ceremonies on major holidays (such as Christmas Day and New Year's Eve) and for major transitions such as baptisms, marriages, and retirements. Why should we not do this for the transition of death?

The friends and relatives of the deceased attend the funeral. But the deceased is left out. Why not begin the ceremony prior to the death so that the central figure can participate and celebrate the life he or she has lived?

Why not attend your own wake?

There is a custom in the academic world that seeks to honor scholars as they approach the end of their careers. Students and colleagues get together and give a series of papers based on the scholar's life-work. These are then published as a celebratory volume, or *festschrift*. Sometimes the papers are presented and the festschrift is published after the person's death, in which case he knows nothing about it. Much better is to have the symposium and publish the papers while the scholar is still alive so that he can appreciate it personally.

Let's do the same for friends and loved ones who are dying.

PLANNING THE CEREMONY

What needs to be decided about your death ceremony? Where to have it, who to have with you, and when to have it are essential considerations for this ceremony.

Where to Have the Ceremony

Where do you want to die? At home or in the hospital, or somewhere else? After my surgeries, it was wonderful to lie in my own bed in my own bedroom. Being home in bed was so much nicer than the hospital room. Yet, if I were severely incapacitated, I might not want to be incontinent at home, soiling my own bed. I might not want my loved ones to have the burden of nursing me if we could not afford to have a professional nurse handle these chores. In this case, I might prefer to die in a hospital or hospice.

There are all kinds of other possibilities—at the beach, in the mountains, or perhaps by a lakeside. When I think about my own death, I imagine that it might be nice to die with a magnificent vista before me—the mountains of the West, a sunset over the Pacific Ocean, among the fjords of Norway, or back home in the land of my birth, England.

A decision such as this might depend on the family's financial ability as well as how we felt physically at the time. Perhaps, therefore, we should plan a few different scenarios and leave the final choice until closer to the time of our death.

Who to Have with Us

Who do we want to be with us as we die? Our spouse or lover? Our parents and children? Friends, but which ones?

I have a friend who, when she is ill, likes to have her partner take care of her and fuss over her. Unfortunately, she married a man who, when he is sick, likes to be left alone. So when he is sick, she fusses over him and annoys him; when she is sick, he leaves her alone and she feels hurt. These two people would probably make very different choices for their death ceremonies.

This part of the process also leads us to consider how we want to end our relationships with each of the people in our lives. Some we remain close to and affectionate with. But there may be friction with others, anger at some, perhaps even a complete break so that we no longer see one another. Is this how we want these relationships to end?

For some the answer may well be yes. If we did not want to ever see a particular person again, we certainly don't want to see him now. But perhaps there are others, from whom we have become alienated or who have become alienated from us, with whom we would like to re-establish a relationship, perhaps even an affectionate one. Now is the time to try this, and if we have managed to find a good counselor to assist us in this process, the counselor might be able to help us bring the relationships into the alignment we seek.

When to Have the Ceremony

The timing of death and suicide can be critical. As we saw in Chapter 13, Mr. L, dying from cancer, decided to live for two more months, and then took his lethal overdose.

Natural deaths take their own course, but the ceremony can be arranged for a time well before death occurs. We might want the ceremony to take place before our pain overwhelms us or before we lapse into a coma. If our death is to be by suicide, we could have a single ceremony that would conclude with our death; alternatively we could have an open ceremony with lots of friends and relatives ahead of time and a more private ceremony for the actual moment of death.

THE CEREMONY ITSELF

This is perhaps the hardest part, but also the part with the most potential. When a wedding is to be arranged, there is a long tradition of how such ceremonies can be staged and many organizations to help us arrange it—churches, caterers, shops to coordinate the gifts, and printers to engrave the invitations. Each organization has years of experience and can present us with many options for its part in the ceremony.

Death ceremonies have rarely been conducted before. Funerals yes, but not ceremonies where the "deceased" is still alive and present. So we have no traditions, and we are on our own. What is it that we want?

A meal, perhaps a feast?
Music, live or recorded?
A somber mood or a boisterous party?
Formal attire or casual dress?
Prayers?
Speeches and toasts?
A planned event or a surprise party?

Ideally, the ceremony should be a *celebration* of the person's life, perhaps where the person tells of his or her most memorable moments, where friends and relatives tell of how they will remember the person, and where the person's life is reviewed.

On the other hand, some lives may have little to celebrate, in which case the mood may be more somber—with feelings of relief to come rather than a review of happiness past. In these cases, talking about the tragedies that the person has encountered might actually be cathartic. Remember, it is the dying person's prerogative to decide on the theme for the ceremony, including whether or not to give it a positive focus.

The dying person might have a private moment with each participant in the ceremony. This would permit a memorable exchange of intimacy between the dying person and those attending the ceremony and give the survivors a special memory to keep.

There is a role here for religion, art, and theater. Moreover, we might benefit from learning about the death rituals of other, especially nonwestern, cultures.

We owe Dr. Jack Kevorkian a great debt for bringing the possibility of assisted suicide to our attention and forcing us to consider the issues. Indeed, I might not have thought about these issues nor written this book had it not been for his provocative actions. However, when I read of his early clients who died in an old Volkswagen van equipped with lethal medications, my first thought was that this was not the way I would commit suicide should I ever choose to do so.

Whatever we may think of the motives and the psychological state of the 38 members of the Heaven's Gate cult who committed suicide at a house in Rancho Santa Fe, California, in early 1997, it is worth noting that their communal death was staged with much forethought. The dress, the method of suicide, and even the way in which the bodies would be positioned, were all carefully planned.

OTHER DEATH CEREMONIES

Elizabeth Cameron has argued that ceremonies can help us in other death-related situations. For those who have survived the suicide of a loved one, she has suggested planning and carrying out a creative ritual to gain social and emotional mastery over the event and to move on with life. She notes that the survivors must be sure that they want to move toward a resolution of the pain and to be ready to let go of the struggle.

The survivor must make choices about the place or places for the ceremony, the clothing and objects to be included, the persons who will attend, a clear statement of purpose (specific enough that it can be written down), and the words and music to be used in the ceremony. Cameron has provided an example of such a ceremony in a recent journal article.

AN EXAMPLE OF A CAREFULLY PLANNED SUICIDE CEREMONY

Jo Roman spent years considering whether rational suicide existed and, after she decided that it did, she thought about how society might assist those who wished to commit suicide to die in a dignified manner. In March 1978, when she was 60, Jo was diagnosed with advanced breast cancer. In June 1979, in line with the principles that she had worked out, Jo killed herself. Jo's experience provides us with an example of a well-planned ceremony for suicide.

Jo had a rich life. Born in 1917, she married just after finishing college, but was widowed soon after when her young husband died of a heart attack. She then went off to Alaska as an interior designer, came back to New York City where she trained as a psychiatric social worker, and eventually married a clinical psychologist, Mel Roman.

In 1975, at the age of 58, Jo began to think about how long she would live and how she might like to die. She considered that a life span of 75 years was sufficient, for after that she might become ill, feeble, and decrepit. So she planned to commit suicide in 1992, and she started a file, adding notes to it regularly. She began to raise the topic of rational suicide with friends and to plan how society might accommodate those who wished to commit suicide. She called her project "*Exit House.*"

When she discussed her ideas with Mel, he was disturbed. The thought of losing Jo when she was 75 and he was only 65 distressed him, and the discussions created a good deal of conflict between them.

In late 1977, Jo's daughter developed breast cancer. Jo helped her through the treatment but, in March 1978, Jo herself was diagnosed with advanced breast cancer, and she moved up the planned date of her suicide to June 1979.

At first Jo kept the information from Mel and others, and she even tried chemotherapy without telling anyone. But eventually the nausea became too severe to hide, and she told Mel in June 1978. Jo decided to live one year of life of good quality without chemotherapy rather than two years of hell with chemotherapy. In retrospect, Jo considered the ten months she spent trying chemotherapy (and suffering the resulting debilitation) a waste of time. Jo killed herself on June 10, 1979, with an overdose of Seconal.

In the preparations for her suicide, Jo, with the assistance of her husband, Mel, reached out to her family and friends. She discussed it in depth with everyone, she wrote her obituary, and she began to write a book, *Exit House,* which would be her legacy to others and which was indeed published after her death. In the final section of that book, Jo brought together her interest in rational suicide, her experiences as a social worker, and her interior design skills to design an Exit House for the future, complete with a description of the legal basis, services provided, and even floor plans for the suites that the suicides would occupy. Alfred Nobel would have been very pleased!

Jo brought up the topic of her suicide with doctors and eventually found one who advised her so that she could decide on a lethal dose of Seconal accompanied by a champagne toast. One doctor offered to give her a lethal injection and two nurses offered to help with the suicide, but Jo declined their assistance. Other doctors offered to sign her death certificate with a cause other than suicide, offers she also declined. She slowly accumulated the Seconal tablets, supposedly as an aid to sleep, and friends provided additional supplies. However, Jo felt strongly that a safe and effective "exit pill" should be developed and sold in drug stores for those who wish to kill themselves. The availability of such a pill might prevent many impulsive suicides since prospective users would know that this option was open to them, and it might also prevent "violent" and bloody suicides.

Jo wished that those who chose rational suicide could have a variety of services available to them: a medical assistant to help with the death itself, a paralegal assistant to help suicides think through and manage the practical issues of ending a life (such as wills and insurance), a protective assistant to prevent people from stumbling across suicides as they lay dying and "saving" them, and personal assistants to be with them on their journey.

The last of these was made available by Jo herself. Jo developed her own circle of assistants and urged other believers in rational suicides to assemble a group early on in the process. She discussed her plans with her friends and family and discovered which of them would assist her. Jo's circle grew to about 100 members. Her hope was that similar support circles could be developed, not centered around only one individual, but available to support anyone in the circle who decided to commit suicide.

In the week before her suicide, Jo and Mel talked—"marathon sessions" is how Mel described them—and they met with family members and close friends. These times were full of tears and laughter. During the final weekend, they made a film in which Jo, Mel, and their intimate friends discussed the issues involved in Jo's impending suicide. Jo also wrote a letter that was mailed to some 300 friends and family members on the day that she killed herself.

Mel notes that the loss of his wife was painful, but the discussions and anticipatory grieving helped him toward recovery. He felt enriched by the experience, as did many of Jo's friends.

Bibliography

I have kept this book relatively free from the scholarly convention of footnoting every scholar and writer whose work is mentioned and whose ideas are used. Nevertheless, these scholars did contribute to the ideas expressed in this book, even though they might not always agree with how their research and writing was applied. The following is a list of those books and articles whose ideas were used in this book.

Alexander, P. (1991). *Rough magic.* New York: Viking.

Beauchamp, T., & Childress, J. (1979). *Principles of biomedical ethics.* New York: Oxford University Press.

Biering-Sorensen, F., Pedersen, W., & Müller, P. G. (1992). Spinal cord injury due to suicide attempts. *Paraplegia, 30,* 139-144.

Binswanger, L. (1958). The case of Ellen West. In R. May, E. Angel & H. F. Ellenberger (Eds.), *Existence* (pp. 237-364). New York: Basic Books.

Brent, D. A., Perper, J., Moritz, G., Allman, C., Friend, A., Schweers, J., Roth, C., Balach, L., & Harrington, K. (1992). Psychiatric effects of exposure to suicide among the friends and acquaintances of adolescent suicide victims. *Journal of the American Academy of Child and Adolescent Psychiatry, 31,* 629-640.

Burns, D. (1980). *Feeling good.* New York: Morrow.

Cameron, E. C. (1991). Creative ritual. *Pastoral Psychology, 40*(1), 3-13.

Cohn, F., Harrold, J., & Lynn, J. (1997). Medical education must deal with end-of-life care. *The Chronicle of Higher Education, 43*(38), A56.

Daeid, N. N. (1997). Suicide in Ireland–1982 to 1992. *Archives of Suicide Research, 3,* 31-42.

DeShano, C. L. (1997). Michigan moves toward better pain management. *Michigan Medicine, 96*(1), 6-21.

Diekstra, R. F. W. (1992). Suicide and euthanasia. *Italian Journal of Suicidology, 2*, 71-78.

Diekstra, R. F. W. (1995). Dying in dignity. *Psychiatry and Clinical Neurosciences, 49*(Suppl. 1), S139-S148.

Ellis, A. (1973). *Humanistic psychotherapy.* New York: Julian.

Fox, D. K. (1997). MSMS, AMA take positive proactive stance—Advocate quality pain management techniques. *Michigan Medicine, 96*(1), 26-27.

Friedman, R. F. (1995). "It's my body and I'll die if I want to." *Journal of Contemporary Health Law and Policy, 12*(1), 183-213.

Frierson, R. L., & Lippman, S. B. (1990). Psychiatric consultation for patients with self-inflicted gunshot wounds. *Psychosomatics, 31*(1), 67-74.

Greenwald, H. (1973). *Direct decision therapy.* San Diego: Edits.

Greenwald, H. (1978). Marie. *Voices, 14*(2), 31-37.

Halleck, S. (1971). *The politics of therapy.* New York: Science House.

Hauerwas, S. (1981). Rational suicide and reasons for living. *Progress in Clinical and Biological Research, 50*, 185-199.

Humphry, D. (1991). *Final exit.* Eugene, OR: Hemlock Society.

Jacobs, J. (1967). A phenomenological study of suicide notes. *Social Problems, 15*, 60-72.

Jezer, M. (1992). *Abbie Hoffman.* New Brunswick, NJ: Rutgers University Press.

Kalish, R. A. (1985). *Death, grief, and caring relationships.* Monterey, CA: Brooks/Cole.

Kelly, G. (1955). *The theory of personal constructs.* New York: Norton.

Kemble, E. C., Birch, F., & Holton, G. (1970). Bridgman, Percy. In C. C. Gillispie (Ed.), *Dictionary of scientific biography* (vol. 2, pp. 457-461). New York: Scribners.

Lester, D. (1969). Suicide as a positive act. *Psychology, 6*(3), 43-48.

Lester, D. (1970). The concept of an appropriate death. *Psychology, 7*(4), 61-66.

Lester, D. (1971). Ellen West's suicide as a case of psychic homicide. *Psychoanalytic Review, 58*, 251-263.

Lester, D. (1988). Suicide and life insurance. *Psychological Reports, 63*, 920.

Lester, D. (1989). *Questions and answers about suicide.* Philadelphia: Charles Press.

Lester, D. (1992). Decriminalization of suicide in Canada and suicide rates. *Psychological Reports, 71*, 738.

Lester, D. (1993). *The cruelest death: The enigma of adolescent suicide.* Philadelphia: Charles Press.

Lester, D. (1993). Decriminalization of suicide in New Zealand and suicide rates. *Psychological Reports, 72*, 1050.

Lester, D. (1994). Bereavement after suicide by firearm. In D. Lester (Ed.), *Suicide '94* (pp. 12-13). Denver: American Association of Suicidology.

Lester, D. (1995). Counseling the suicidal person in the modern age. *Crisis Intervention and Time-Limited Treatment, 2,* 159-165.

Lester, D. (1996). Psychological issues in euthanasia, suicide, and assisted suicide. *Journal of Social Issues, 52*(2), 51-62.

Lester, D. (1996-1997). AIDS and rational suicide. *Omega, 34,* 333-336.

Lester, D. (1997). Easing the legacy of suicide. *Changes, 15,* 134-139.

Lester, D. (1997). *Making sense of suicide: An in-depth look at why people kill themselves.* Philadelphia: Charles Press.

Lester, D. (1997). The sexual politics of double suicide. *Feminism & Psychology, 7,* 148-154.

Lester, D., & Brockopp, G. W. (Eds.) (1973). *Crisis intervention and counseling by telephone.* Springfield, IL: Charles Thomas.

Lucas, C., & Seiden, H. M. (1987). *Silent grief.* New York: Scribners.

McDowell, C. P., Rothberg, J. M., & Koshes, R. J. (1994). Witnessed suicides. *Suicide and Life-Threatening Behavior, 24,* 213-223.

Middlebrook, D. W. (1991). *Anne Sexton.* Boston: Houghton-Mifflin.

Pretzel, P. W. (1968, July). Philosophical and ethical considerations of suicide prevention. *Bulletin of Suicidology,* 30-38.

Quill, T. E. (1993). "Doctor, I want to die. Will you help me?" *Journal of the American Medical Association, 270,* 870-873.

Rollin, B. (1985). *Last wish.* New York: Simon & Schuster.

Roman, J. (1980). *Exit house.* New York: Seaview Books.

Rudestam, K. E. (1990). Survivors of suicide. In D. Lester (Ed.), *Current concepts of suicide* (pp. 203-213). Philadelphia: Charles Press.

Seiden, R. H. (1986). Self-deliverance or self-destruction? *Euthanasia Review, 1*(1), 48-56.

Shneidman, E. S. (1967). Sleep and self-destruction. In E. S. Shneidman (Ed.), *Essays in self-destruction* (pp. 510-539). New York: Science House.

Shneidman, E. S. (1996). *The suicidal mind.* New York: Oxford University Press.

Shneidman, E. S., & Farberow, N. L. (1970). The logic of suicide. In E. S. Shneidman, N. L. Farberow, & R. E. Litman (Eds.), *The psychology of suicide* (pp. 63-71). New York: Science House.

Sohlman, R. (1962). Alfred Nobel and the Nobel Foundation. In H. Schuck (Ed.), *Nobel: The man and his prizes* (pp. 15-72). Amsterdam: Elsevier.

Stone, G. (1999). *Suicide and attempted suicide.* New York: Carroll & Graf.

Thomas, D. (1971). *The poems of Dylan Thomas.* New York: New Directions.

Victoroff, V. M. (1983). *The suicidal patient.* Oradell, NJ: Medical Economics Books.

Weisman, A., & Hackett, T. P. (1961). Predilection to death. *Psychosomatic Medicine, 23,* 232-256.

Wertheimer, A. (1991). *A special scar.* Philadelphia: Brunner-Routledge.

White-Bowden, S. (1985). *Everything to live for.* New York: Poseidon.

Wilber, C. G. (1987). Some thoughts on suicide: Is it logical? *American Journal of Forensic Medicine and Pathology, 8,* 302-308.

Yeh, B. Y., & Lester, D. (1987). An economic model for suicide. In D. Lester, *Suicide as a learned behavior* (pp. 51-57). Springfield, IL: Charles Thomas.

Index

Psychiatric/psychological disorders
and personal decision to
commit suicide, 29–31
See also Rationality and suicide
Psychoanalytic theory, 35, 38
Psychological death, 23–24
Psychology Today, 46
Psychosemantic fallacy, 39–40
Psychotherapy, 14, 32–33
Public demand for assisted suicide,
49

Quality of life, 11, 43–44

Rarity of suicide, 34–35
Rationality and suicide
autonomous individuals, 37
defining terms, 31–33
economic view of suicide, 38–39
emotional *vs.* rational suicide, 37
empirical judgments of
rationality, 36–37
laws, does suicide follow rational,
38–39
logical thinking, 39–40
precipitates a suicide, what?, 35
psychiatrically disturbed people's
ability to have rational
premises, 29–31, 33–34
rarity of suicide, statistical,
34–35
summary/review, 40–41
unconscious forces, 35–36
See also Death ceremony
Religion, 55
Richard Stockton College of New
Jersey, 9
Right-to-die organizations, 16, 76
Roe vs. Wade, 61
Role playing, 82
Rollin, Betty, 92, 93
Roman, Jo, 103–105

Saathoff, Mary A., 48
Samaritans, The, 15
Schur, Max, 37
Seconal, 104
Serotonin reuptake inhibitor (SRI),
46
Sexton, Anne, 46–47
Sexual problems and
antidepressants, 46
Shneidman, Edwin, 38, 39, 51
Shock after loved one commits
suicide, 68, 97
Silent Grief (Lucas & Seiden), 71
Simultaneous occurrence of
different kinds of death,
23–24
Social death, 23–24
Special Scar, A (Wertheimer), 71
Speijer, Nico, 6–7
Statistics on suicide, 4, 31, 34–35
Subjective definition of normality,
35
Suicide and Attempted Suicide
(Stone), 3
Suicide notes, 73–74
Suicide Prevention and Crisis
Service, 9
Survivors groups, 15, 70–71

Telephone counseling, 9
Terminal illness, suicide when
suffering from, 50
Thomas, Dylan, 26
Time magazine, 11, 46
Timing of death, 27–28
Trauma suffered by family/loved
ones, 89–91
Traumatic experiences in childhood
and suicide decisions, 30

Unconscious forces and rationality
of suicide, 35–36